Praise for the 3rd Edition of Lean UX

"For the past eight years, *Lean UX* has been my go-to recommendation for teams learning how to work together to design great experiences. This latest version goes above and beyond, solidifying the teachings in an easy-to-follow format and examples of this working in practice. This is required reading for any modern product development team."

Melissa Perri, CEO, Produx Labs,
Senior Lecturer, Harvard Business School

"*Lean UX* was such an influential book in my career, and I was thrilled to read the newest edition. Jeff and Josh continue to push these ideas forward by putting them into practice."

David J. Bland, author of *Testing Business Ideas*

"As the Siskel and Ebert of the digital product-making process, Gothelf and Seiden provide scathingly precise guidance to large organizations undergoing their digital transformations. From their combined experience in the field spanning the spryest tech startup to century-spanning grown-up companies, their guidance is refreshingly more 'let's fix this now' painkiller advice from real practitioners than the latest homeotherapy cure-all from armchair agilists."

John Maeda, SVP Chief Experience Officer, Everbridge

Praise for Previous Editions of Lean UX

"The quality of the user experience has become the most important differentiator for a company's product. In *Lean UX*, Josh Seiden and Jeff Gothelf highlight the methods and strategies for ensuring that great experiences are built with as little waste as possible in a collaborative, cross-functional effort. It is a must-read not just for designers but for everyone on the team, from executive leadership to intern."

Tom Boates, Founder/CEO of Brilliant

"If you're struggling to ship winning user experiences with Agile development methods, get this book! Jeff and Josh share proven methods for creative ideation, planning, and problem-solving without heavy deliverable baggage. The new edition brings some crucial updates, including help with designing and tracking experiments, and refinements to many of the critical tools of Lean UX."

Christian Crumlish, VP Product, 7cups.com; coauthor of
Designing Social Interfaces, **Second Edition**

"In the time since *Lean UX* was first published, the practices it outlines have become widespread. The revised and expanded *Lean UX*, second edition, will show you how to apply Lean UX thinking to both green fields and sustaining innovation projects, create the right company culture for success, and inspire you with new case studies of Lean UX in practice."

Lane Goldstone, Cofounder, Brooklyn Copper Cookware

"In a very short time span, Lean UX went from an obscure idea to a transformative way of building and delivering products that meet the customer's needs. It's now a critical approach to design and needs to be top of mind for every designer, developer, and product manager."

Jared Spool, Cofounder, Center Centre UX Design School

"Approachable, actionable advice from two people that have been 'getting out of the building' and evolving Lean UX globally for over a decade. In sharing that experience, this book moves beyond theory and brings insights from real work done, providing context-rich narratives to digest and fuel UX teams working in tandem with the Agile software development process."

Courtney Hemphill, Partner at Carbon Five

"Customer development and Lean Startup changed the way businesses are built, because even the smartest teams can't predict market and user behavior. This book brings both methodologies to UX so you can build cheaper, faster, and—most importantly—better experiences."

Alex Osterwalder, author and entrepreneur;
Cofounder, Business Model Foundry GmbH

"There is a revolution afoot. It is the move away from big design up front and isolated, specialized teams throwing documents over the wall to each other. Applying the principles of Lean Startups, Jeff and Josh lay out the principles of Lean UX, which can literally transform the way you bring experiences to life. I have firsthand experience applying their wisdom and am excited about taking Agile to the next level. Get this book. But most importantly, put this book into practice."

Bill Scott, Sr. Director, User Interface Engineering, PayPal, Inc.

"While there is no question that great product teams must put user experience design front and center, many teams have struggled to reconcile the techniques and objectives of user experience design with the rhythm and pace of modern Agile development teams. Lean UX is the collection of techniques and mindset that I advocate to modern product teams that know they need the benefits of both."

Marty Cagan, Founder, Silicon Valley Product Group;
former SVP Product and Design, eBay

"Jeff and Josh's passion for getting UX (and, really, all of product development) right comes across powerfully in this detailed yet eminently readable book. The case studies, examples, and research serve to highlight the power of building a Lean UX process, and there's a great deal of actionable advice taken from these. I'm ordering a copy for everyone on our design, UX, and product teams at Moz."

Rand Fishkin, CEO and Cofounder, Moz

"A fantastic combination of case studies and practical advice that your team can use today. Whether you're at a startup or a Fortune 500 company, this book will change the way you build products."

Laura Klein, author of UX *for Lean Startups*

"*Lean UX* provides a prescriptive framework for how to build better products, moving design away from pixel perfection for the sake of it toward iterative learning, smarter effort, and outcome-based results. Product managers, business owners, and startup employees—along with designers— can benefit greatly from *Lean UX*."

Ben Yoskovitz, Founding Partner, Highline BETA

THIRD EDITION

Lean UX

Designing Great Products with Agile Teams

Jeff Gothelf and Josh Seiden

Beijing · Boston · Farnham · Sebastopol · Tokyo

Lean UX

by Jeff Gothelf and Josh Seiden

Copyright © 2021 Gothelf Corp. and Seiden Consulting, Inc. All rights reserved.

Printed in Canada.

Published by O'Reilly Media, Inc., 1005 Gravenstein Highway North, Sebastopol, CA 95472.

O'Reilly books may be purchased for educational, business, or sales promotional use. Online editions are also available for most titles (*http://oreilly.com*). For more information, contact our corporate/institutional sales department: 800-998-9938 or *corporate@oreilly.com*.

Acquisitions Editor: Jennifer Pollock	**Indexer:** Sue Klefstad
Development Editor: Angela Rufino	**Interior Designer:** David Futato
Production Editor: Christopher Faucher	**Cover Designer:** Kenn Vondrak
Copyeditor: nSight, Inc.	**Illustrator:** Kate Dullea
Proofreader: Sonia Saruba	

March 2013:	First Edition
September 2016:	Second Edition
September 2021:	Third Edition

Revision History for the Third Edition
2021-07-28:   First Release
2021-12-03:   Second Release

See *http://oreilly.com/catalog/errata.csp?isbn=9781098116309* for release details.

978-1-098-11630-9

[MBP]

For Carrie, Grace, and Sophie

...and Vicky, Naomi, Amanda, and Joey.

Contents

PART I: INTRODUCTION AND PRINCIPLES

PART II: PROCESS

PART III: COLLABORATION

PART IV: LEAN UX IN YOUR ORGANIZATION

Forewords

In reading *Lean UX*, you're about to embark on a tour of a new way of working. For those of us steeped in traditional management techniques, it may seem a little disorienting. I sometimes like to imagine what it would be like to have a bird's-eye view of the typical modern corporation. From on high, in your mind's eye you could examine each silo of functional excellence one at a time: Marketing, Operations, Manufacturing, IT, Engineering, Design, and on and on in a tidy row of crisp, well-run silos.

Let's imagine you reached down to grab one of these silos and popped its top off to see inside. What would you see? This being a modern company, you'd see each silo designed for maximum efficiency. To achieve this efficiency, you'd likely find a highly iterative, customer-centric approach to problem-solving. In Manufacturing, you'd encounter traditional Lean thinking. In Engineering or IT, perhaps some variation on Agile development. In Marketing, customer development. In Operations, DevOps. And of course in Design, the latest in design thinking, interaction design, and user research techniques.

Zooming back out to our high perch, we might be forgiven for thinking, "This company uses a variety of rigorous, hypothesis-driven, customer-centric, and iterative methodologies. Surely, it must be an extremely agile company, capable of reacting quickly to changes in market conditions and continuously innovating!" But those of us who work in modern companies know how far this is from the truth.

How is it possible that our departmental silos are operating with agility but our companies are hopelessly rigid and slow? From our far-off vantage point, we have missed something essential. Although our departments may value agility, the *interconnections* between them are still mired in an antiquated industrial past.

Consider just one example, which I hope will sound familiar. A company decides it must innovate to survive. It commissions a design team (either in-house or external) to investigate the future of its industry and recommend innovative new products that could secure its future. A period of great excitement commences. Customers are interviewed, observed, analyzed.

Experiments, surveys, focus groups, prototypes, and smoke tests follow one after the other. Concepts are rapidly conceived, tested, rejected, and refined.

And what happens at the end of this process? The designers proudly present—and the business enthusiastically celebrates—a massive specification document with their findings and recommendations. The iteration, experimentation, and discovery ceases. Now Engineering is called upon to execute this plan. And although the engineering process may be agile, the specification document is rigidly fixed. What happens if the engineers discover that the specification was unworkable or even slightly flawed? What if the concepts worked great in the lab but have no commercial appeal? What if market conditions have changed since the original "learning" took place?

I once spoke to a company that had commissioned—at terrible expense—a multiyear study of their industry. The result was an impressive "view of the future" display custom-built into their corporate headquarters. Inside this room, you could see an extrapolation of what the next 10 years would look like in their industry, complete with working demos of futuristic product concepts. You can guess what happened over the succeeding 10 years: absolutely nothing. The company rotated hundreds or thousands of executives, managers, and workers through this glimpse of the future. And in fact, 10 years later, the room no longer looks futuristic. Against all odds, their forecasts turned out to be largely accurate. And yet, the company had failed to commercialize even one of the recommendations in the attendant specification document. So I asked the company what they planned to do next. They told me they were going back to the original designers and asking them to forecast the next 10 years! The company blamed their engineers and managers, not the designers, for their failure to commercialize.

When I tell this story to nondesigners, they are horrified and want to convince me that it is the fancy design firm that is to blame. When I tell it to senior executives—in both large companies and startups alike—they cringe. They are constantly deluged with complaints from every single function that they are fast and cutting edge, but it is the other departments that slow the company down. When the whole company fails to find new sources of growth, there is plenty of blame to go around.

But the fault is not with the designers, the engineers, or even the executives. The problem is the systems we use to build companies. We are still building linear organizations in a world that demands constant change. We are still building silos in a world that demands thorough collaboration. And we are still investing in analysis, arguing over specifications, and efficiently producing deliverables in a world that demands continuous experimentation in order to achieve continuous innovation.

When this book first came out in 2012, it was still early days for Lean Startup. It's now been fifteen years since I first began writing and speaking about what was then a very new concept, and 2021 is also the tenth anniversary of the publication of *The Lean Startup: How Today's Entrepreneurs Use Continuous Innovation to Achieve Radically Successful Businesses* (Crown Business, 2011). In that time, I have seen the ideas grow and spread—from industry to industry, sector to sector, and function to function. Every time we have encountered new terrain, we have relied on farsighted leaders to help translate the core principles and develop new processes to implement them. We've learned an enormous amount about how it can be used, and practitioners all over the world have contributed new tools and methods.

Lean UX is an important step in that evolution. And thanks to Jeff Gothelf and Josh Seiden's commitment to continuing to advance the discipline, this new edition builds on what was already a comprehensive look at how Lean Startup principles apply in a design context. The fundamental tools and techniques it introduces for achieving superior collaboration, faster delivery, and— most importantly—dramatically better products have been augmented to include newer entries like the Lean UX Canvas and Hypothesis Prioritization Canvas. There's more on the relationship between Lean UX and story mapping, too, as well as on design sprints.

Lean Startup is a big tent. It builds on established ideas from many disciplines, from Lean manufacturing to design thinking. It gives us a common vocabulary and set of concepts that can be used to accelerate results across the whole company. We can stop wasting time arguing about who is to blame and which department should rule the day.

It is my hope that all of us will remember to heed Jeff's call to "get out of the deliverables business" and return our focus to where it belongs, enlisting the whole corporation in its most urgent task: delighting customers.

It is time to break down the silos, unite the clans, and get to work.

—Eric Ries
July 28, 2021
San Francisco, CA

This edition of *Lean UX* is a timely contribution to the evolving world of design, entrepreneurship, and innovation. Ten years ago, part of our work with companies involved having to convince leaders of the value of innovation beyond their core business. This debate has now mostly gone away. Corporate leaders are now convinced that innovation is the best way to drive long-term growth within their companies.

While leaders now see the value of innovation, a different challenge still remains. Very few leaders are satisfied with their company's innovation performance. It appears that a lot of the work that innovation teams do does not follow a repeatable process. This is the question that leaders now consistently ask us: what are the structures and processes they need to put in place to have repeatable innovation?

This is what makes this edition of *Lean UX* so timely. We believe that innovation is a profession, not simply a calling for the chosen few. In order to professionalize innovation, we need to develop the right tools and processes for innovators to use in their day-to-day work. As people learn to use these tools, they will then be able to produce repeatable value for their organizations. This is the ongoing contribution that *Lean UX* is making.

Even after the publication of the first edition of *Lean UX*, the biggest lie in software and product development is still phase two. The idea is that teams should be allowed to execute on whatever they have on their road map and then deal with any customer issues after launching (i.e., in the second version of the product). The problem is that we never get to phase two, and flawed products remain in the market. This is probably why 7 out of 10 new product launches flop.

So how do we solve this challenge? First, we need to develop tools that fit the nature of innovation. *Lean UX* is based on the clear understanding that innovation is not a technological or execution challenge. Instead, the challenge for teams is to search for value propositions that resonate with customers and for business models that are profitable.

Such searching requires that teams navigate complexity and uncertainty. This is not a linear process based on simple cause and effect. It is a nonlinear process. *Lean UX* provides ways for teams to navigate this complexity by moving iteratively and creatively through the murky waters of innovation until they find something that works.

We once worked with a leader who kept asking his teams to bring him 10x ideas. We tried to gently remind the leader that it would be impossible for him and his team to identify a 10x idea on day one. Leaders cannot pick winning ideas; they can only create the context in which the best ideas emerge. By following the process laid out in *Lean UX*, teams can work together to quickly sketch out and test their business ideas. The winning ideas will emerge through that testing and iteration.

The complexity of innovation also means that teams cannot navigate their way to success without collaborating with colleagues from various key functions. There is quite a distance to travel between having an idea and then designing, testing, and launching that idea into the market. Such work requires crossfunctional collaboration. The challenge is that a lot of organizations still maintain the silos and handoffs that kill the ability of teams to collaborate.

We have worked with several organizations where innovation teams need to get the approval of legal and compliance to run experiments. At one such organization, it took over two months for a simple Wizard of Oz experiment to be approved. *Lean UX* describes practical ways that can be used to overcome such barriers to innovation.

Even after the product launches, the mindset articulated in *Lean UX* helps teams to continue sketching and testing. It is critical that teams don't treat the launch of a product as the end of the process. It is critical that they continue to improve their offering using Lean UX methods. It is important to always remember that companies are not in the business of deliverables; they are in the business of delighting customers!

We hope that you not only enjoy reading this wonderful book, but that you also take the lessons and apply them to your day-to-day work.

—Alex Osterwalder
May 30, 2021
Lausanne, Switzerland

—Tendayi Viki
May 30, 2021
Harare, Zimbabwe

Authors' Note

As we set out to write the third edition of this book, we realized that the influence of an ever-diverse group of practitioners, writers, coaches, and consultants has helped Lean UX grow and evolve to meet the changing needs of software design and development. We wanted to take a moment to thank them.

We continue to learn from the core group of colleagues and fellow road warriors who share their wisdom and feedback with us, including Tendayi Viki, Teresa Torres, Melissa Perri, Hope Gurion, Barry O'Reilly, Sam McAfee, Andy Polaine, David Bland, Andi Plantenberg, Jonathan Bertfield, Kate Leto, Daniel Stillman, Beth Temple, Jocelyn Miller, Bob Gower, David Bland, Douglas Ferguson, Martina Hodges-Schell, Erin Stadler, Jeff Patton, Petra Wille, Janet Bumpas, Jonathan Berger, and Adrian Howard. We build our ideas on top of theirs and those of our clients.

As always, we would like to thank the many folks who have contributed material, stories, research leads, Twitter help, technical wisdom, and emotional support to the book. In particular, we'd like to thank Andrew Bourne, Ike Breed, Steven Cohn, Regine Gilbert, Victor M. Gonzalez, Zach Gottlieb, Jamila Isoke, Liz Laub, Jon Loyens, Dan Maccarone, Jono Mallanyk, Lin Nie, Greg Petroff, Steve Portigal, Leisa Reichelt, Delphine Sassi, Alexander Schardt, Kristin Skinner, Erik Skogsberg, Jessica Tiao, Kate Towsey, Ben Walker, Rosie Webster, and Lee Weiss.

We're grateful to the team at Scrum.org, including Dave West, Steve Porter, Erik Weber, and Gary Pedretti, and all of the professional Scrum trainers we met there who helped bring our work to the Scrum community and who helped us sharpen our understanding of the needs of that community.

Thanks to Eric Ries for continuing to support the work of *Lean UX* and the other authors and titles in the Lean Series, and to Melissa Duffield, Angela Rufino, Mary Treseler, and Jennifer Pollock at O'Reilly, who continue to make it possible for this book to succeed.

Finally, we'd be remiss if we didn't thank the members of the Balanced Team working group, where we first started workshopping these ideas all those years ago. We're grateful to Lane Goldstone for being the catalyst and driving force in bringing that group together and bringing so many wonderful people together. In particular, we owe a debt of gratitude to Janice Fraser, who first introduced us to the ideas of Lean Startup and who coined the phrase "Lean UX."

Note: From Jeff

As our partnership enters its second decade, I continue to see Josh as a friend, collaborator, and logical sounding board. The way we practice these ideas is different from the days we first started doing it, but as the needs of the market and the realities of the world change, we continue to work together to find new ways to bring better ways of working to the corporate world. I'm grateful for that and for his relentless pursuit of the perfect homemade sourdough and corned beef.

As always, none of this happens without family support and love. Carrie, Grace, and Sophie continue to indulge my work, my writing, and my dad jokes. I couldn't ask for more. I love you all. Thank you.

Note: From Josh

In this book, Jeff and I describe a working style that is deeply collaborative. That's my preferred style of working—I always feel that I learn more and am more effective when I'm collaborating. Whatever I've been able to contribute to this book is a result of the amazing collaborations I've been lucky enough to enjoy in my career. You all know who you are. I'm very grateful to all of you.

There is one working collaboration that I do need to call out, though: it's been a real pleasure to continue to collaborate with Jeff. Jeff supplies many of the things in this partnership that I can't, including optimism about deadlines, audacity in setting goals, and tirelessness in evangelizing. He's a smart, hard-working, and egoless partner. He is not, however, funny. If that's needed, I usually have to provide it.

Thanks, finally, to Vicky, Naomi, and Amanda. I love you.

From Jeff and Josh

Another five years have passed since we last updated this book. We continue to be in awe of the community and the work that the ideas in this book have spawned. So much has changed, and yet so many of the problems that software design and development teams face remain the same. The challenge has always been to build not only broader cross-functional collaboration but a continuous conversation with the customer that influences what work we choose to do. The good news is that, with the deeper assimilation of Agile and Scrum, along with the goal-setting framework of objectives and key results (OKRs), organizations are taking an even closer look at how to become nimbler and more customer-centric. We, too, have learned how the techniques in *Lean UX* can be applied even more effectively. We're excited to share that with you.

Every time we teach Lean UX or use it in our daily work, we learn a better way to apply it. We try something new, inspect it, adapt from the learning, and update our thinking. We suspect you're doing the same thing, and we'd love to hear about it.

Please keep in touch with us and share your thoughts. You can reach us at *jeff@jeffgothelf.com* and *josh@joshuaseiden.com*. We always look forward to hearing from you.

Preface

The biggest lie in software is *still* phase two.

If you've spent any time building digital products in the past 30 years—regardless of your role—you've felt the sting of this lie. And if your team claims to be agile, is phase two still a valid concept? Teams prioritize features and ideas for each sprint, racing toward a launch date while pushing nonprioritized ideas to the next phase of work. Except that phase never comes, and those features are gone—never to be heard from again. As designers, product managers, coaches, and consultants, we've had hundreds, if not thousands, of wireframes, product backlog items, and workflows end up in this same bucket.

But were these ideas abandoned because they were flawed? Because something changed in the market? Did the features that shipped actually meet customer and business goals? Or did the team simply forget? They never got to phase two.

In *The Lean Startup*, Eric Ries lays out his vision for how to ensure the ideas that have the most value get the most resources. The method Ries promotes relies on experimentation, rapid iterations of ideas, and evolutionary processes. In a truly agile environment, teams launch features continuously, making the actual deployment of code a nonevent. The entire concept of phase two has become moot.

The junction of Lean Startup and user experience (UX) design—and their symbiotically beneficial coexistence—is *Lean UX*.

What Is Lean UX?

The Lean principles underlying Lean Startup apply to Lean UX in three ways. First, they help us remove waste from our UX design process. We do just enough work—be it design, research, writing, whatever—to move the conversation between design, development, and product forward. These minimally viable conversations move us away from the lengthy negotiations triggered by heavily documented handoffs. Instead, a Lean UX process creates only the design artifacts we need to move the team's *learning* forward. Second, Lean principles drive us to harmonize our "system" of designers, developers, product managers, quality assurance engineers, marketers, and others in a transparent, cross-functional collaboration that brings nondesigners into our design process. Lean UX is a transparent process that not only reveals what designers do but encourages participation from everyone on the team.

Last, and perhaps most important, is the mindset shift we gain from adopting a model based on experimentation and validated learning. Instead of relying on any one person—a hero designer, the lead engineer, a business stakeholder —to divine the best solution from a single point of view, we use rapid experimentation and measurement to take an outside-in view of the experience we're creating. We push to learn quickly—to discover—how well (or poorly) our ideas meet the needs of our customers. In all of this, the designer's role begins to evolve beyond just creation of artifacts toward design facilitation—and with that, we take on a new set of responsibilities.

Besides Lean Startup, Lean UX has two other foundations: *design thinking* and *Agile* development philosophies. Design thinking helps us widen the scope of our work beyond interfaces and artifacts. Design thinking looks at systems and helps us apply design tools to broader problems. It relies on collaboration, iteration, making, and empathy as core to problem-solving. Perhaps the biggest takeaway from design thinking is its focus on building empathy—teamwide— for the end user. Practicing Lean UX means the entire team builds this empathy. Agile refocuses software development on shorter cycles, regular delivery of value, and continuous learning. It seeks to get ideas (oftentimes as working software) to customers quickly, sense how these ideas are received, and respond frequently to new learning along the way. As the Scrum guide puts it: inspect and adapt.

Lean UX uses these foundations to bridge the speed of Agile and the need for design in the product-development life cycle. If you've struggled to figure out how UX design can work in Agile environments, Lean UX is the answer.

Lean UX breaks down the barriers that have kept software designers isolated from real business needs on the one hand and actual implementation on the other. Lean UX not only brings designers to the table, but it brings our partners in product management, business, and technology to the whiteboard to work with us on the best solutions in an ongoing way.

Early in his career, Jeff worked with a large pharmaceutical client who had hired the agency he worked for to redesign their ecommerce platform. The goal was to increase revenues by 15%. Jeff was the lead interaction designer on the team. In the vacuum of their office, Jeff and his team spent months researching the current system, supply chain, competitors, target audience, and contextual use scenarios. They researched personas and assembled strategic models. Jeff designed a new information architecture for the product catalog and crafted a brand-new shopping and checkout experience.

The project took months. And when the work was complete, the team packaged it all up into a PowerPoint slide deck. This was a formidable deck—and it had to be, considering the $600,000 price tag! The team went over to the client's office and spent an entire eight-hour day going over each and every pixel and word in that deck. When it was over, the client clapped. (They really did.) Jeff and the team were relieved. The client loved the work. And Jeff's team never looked at that deck again.

Six months after that meeting, nothing had changed on the client's site. The client never looked at that deck again, either.

The moral of this story: building a pixel-perfect specification might be a route to rake in six-figure consulting fees, but it's not a way to make a meaningful difference to a real product that is crucial to real users. It's also not the reason that any designer got into the product design business. We got in it to build valuable products and services, not to write specs.

When we practice Lean UX, we ensure we're solving a real problem for real customers in a meaningful way. Some teams we work with today create entirely new products or services. They are not working within an existing product framework or structure. In "greenfield" projects like these, we are simultaneously trying to discover how this new product or service will be used, how it will behave, and how we are going to build it. Most importantly, we want to validate that it's solving a meaningful problem for its intended target audience. This is an environment of continual change, and there isn't a lot of time or patience for planning or up-front design.

Other teams work with established products that were created with traditional design and development methods. Their challenge is different. The systems they work on were developed to meet the needs of a specific period of time. The rapid pace of change in the market means that those needs have likely evolved. These teams need to optimize these existing platforms to meet new realities while increasing revenue and brand value. They usually have more resources at their disposal than a ground-floor startup, but they still have to use their resources efficiently—discovering the best way to spend those resources to build products and services their customers actually want.

Perhaps one of the toughest changes Lean UX asks us to make is to overcome the feeling that we are showing work in an "unfinished" or "ugly" state. Even today, after nearly 15 years of working this way, we still struggle with this one. We've learned over the years that our first attempt will inevitably require revision. So the sooner we get our ideas out, the sooner we can figure out what those revisions should be. Waiting too long to get that feedback is wasteful. We invest too much in the initial design and are less flexible to changes because of the effort we've already put in. The sooner we learn what changes need to be made, the less we've invested in the current idea. It will hurt less to change course. Accepting the iterative nature of design and, more broadly, software requires the support of a high-functioning, humble, collaborative team. You need to know—as a team—that you're *not* going to get it right the first time and that you're all working together to iterate your way forward. The deployment of the code is not the measure of a Lean UX team's success. It's the positive impact you have on your customers.

There are many elements that affect the success of digital systems. Design is certainly an important component, but product management, engineering, marketing, legal, compliance, and copywriting (to name a few) all have an impact on the system. No one discipline has all the answers. To that end, no one point of view has all the answers, either. The greater the diversity of your team—gender diversity, racial diversity, etc.—the more innovative and broad-reaching the solutions the team generates. Inclusivity is key to a successful collaboration. This is the nature of our digital medium. Broad collaboration creates better work. Revision and iteration make for better products. Within the pages of this book, we've distilled the insights and tactics that have allowed us to adopt this point of view and to create real success for product and business teams—and real satisfaction for customers.

Who Is Lean UX For?

This book is, first, for product designers who know they can contribute more and be more effective with their teams. That said, we believe that "user experience" is the sum total of all of the interactions that a user has with your product and service. It's created by all of the decisions that you and your team make about that product or service. It's not just user interface or functionality. It's also about pricing, purchasing experience, onboarding, support, etc. In other words, user experience is created by the whole team. For that reason, this book is also for product managers who need better ways to define their products with their teams and to validate them with their customers. It's also for Scrum masters and developers who understand that a collaborative, agile team environment leads to better code and more meaningful work. And, finally, it's for managers—managers of UX teams, project teams, business lines, departments, and companies—who understand the difference a great UX can make.

What's in It for You?

The book is set up in four sections.

Part I, "Introduction and Principles", provides an overview and introduction to Lean UX and its founding principles. We lay out the reasons the evolution of the UX design process is so critical and describe Lean UX. We also discuss the underlying principles that you'll need to understand to make Lean UX successful in your Agile work environments.

Part II, "Process", introduces the Lean UX canvas and walk through each of its eight steps. We also share examples of how we and others have done these things in the past.

Part III, "Collaboration", takes a deep look at collaboration between designers and other disciplines, and introduces tools and case studies to bring together several popular ways of working, like design sprints, design systems, and collaborative research with Lean UX. Finally, we share some considerations for better integrating Lean UX into the rhythms of an Agile process.

Part IV, "Lean UX in Your Organization", tackles the integration of Lean UX practices into your organization. We discuss the organizational shifts that need to take place at the corporate level, team level, and individual contributor level for these ideas to truly take hold.

Our hope is that this book will continue to serve as a way forward for UX designers, their colleagues, and product teams in all organizations still waiting for "phase two." Although the book is filled with tactics and techniques to help develop your processes, we'd like you to remember that Lean UX is, at its core, a mindset.

—Jeff and Josh

O'Reilly Online Learning

——— NOTE ———

For more than 40 years, *O'Reilly Media* has provided technology and business training, knowledge, and insight to help companies succeed.

Our unique network of experts and innovators share their knowledge and expertise through books, articles, and our online learning platform. O'Reilly's online learning platform gives you on-demand access to live training courses, in-depth learning paths, interactive coding environments, and a vast collection of text and video from O'Reilly and 200+ other publishers. For more information, visit *http://oreilly.com*.

How to Contact Us

Please address comments and questions concerning this book to the publisher:

O'Reilly Media, Inc.
1005 Gravenstein Highway North
Sebastopol, CA 95472
800-998-9938 (in the United States or Canada)
707-829-0515 (international or local)
707-829-0104 (fax)

We have a web page for this book, where we list errata, examples, and any additional information. You can access this page at *https://oreil.ly/lean-UX-3e*.

Email *bookquestions@oreilly.com* to comment or ask technical questions about this book.

Visit *http://oreilly.com* for news and information about our books and courses.

Find us on Facebook: *http://facebook.com/oreilly*

Follow us on Twitter: *http://twitter.com/oreillymedia*

Watch us on YouTube: *http://youtube.com/oreillymedia*

INTRODUCTION AND PRINCIPLES

About Part I

In this first part, we provide an introduction to Lean UX and its founding principles. We discuss why the evolution of the product design and development process is so critical, and we describe what Lean UX is. We also discuss the underlying principles you'll need to understand to make Lean UX work in your organization.

Chapter 1, "More Important Now than Ever Before", provides a brief history of product design and development and why it's time for that process to evolve.

In Chapter 2, "Principles", we present a detailed look at the key principles that drive the Lean UX process. These principles offer a framework for a leaner product design and discovery process, and also provide basic management guidelines for these teams. They are critical to the success of Lean UX and, if incorporated into your organization, will have a profound impact on your culture and on the productivity and success of your teams.

Chapter 3, "Outcomes", is focused on the idea of outcomes, which have always been an important concept in Lean UX, but over the years, we've developed new ways of thinking about and working with them. Because outcomes are so critical to Lean UX, we've expanded our discussion of this concept. This chapter shares with you our current understanding of the idea.

CHAPTER 1

More Important Now than Ever Before

It's not iteration if you do it only once.
Jeff Patton

Design Is Always Evolving

When designers first brought their craft to software in the '80s and '90s, they approached the work in the same way they approached the earlier materials they worked with. In industrial design, print design, fashion design, or any field involving physical outputs, the manufacturing step is a critical constraint. When designing for physical materials, designers need to figure out what they're making *before* they begin production, because production is expensive. It's expensive to set up a factory floor to produce hard goods or garments. It's expensive to set up a printing press for a print run.

Working in software, designers faced new challenges. They had to figure out the grammar of this new medium, and as they did, they saw new specialties like interaction design and information architecture emerge. But the *process* by which designers practiced remained mostly unquestioned. Designers still designed products in great detail in advance, because they still had to deal with a "manufacturing" process: the work had to be duplicated onto floppy disks and CDs, which were then distributed to market in exactly the same way that physical goods were distributed. The cost of getting it wrong remained high. Paradoxically, though, this way of working didn't really prevent anyone from getting it wrong. Too often, designers worked in isolation—siloed—before passing their work to developers, who in turn worked in a silo before passing the work on to QA, and so on. And everyone was working with limited market feedback.

Today, we face a new reality. Software production has become continuous. The internet has changed the way we distribute software. The proliferation of mobile devices, wearables, and the Internet of Things has changed the way we consume it. We are no longer limited by a physical manufacturing process, and we are able to get our digital products and services into customers' hands at a pace unheard of just a few years ago.

This changes everything.

Teams now are facing intense pressure from competitors who are using techniques like Agile software development, continuous integration, and continuous deployment to radically reduce their cycle times. Take Amazon as an example. *The ecommerce giant pushes new code live to their customers every single second of every minute.*[1] And they are using these short cycles as a competitive advantage—releasing early and often, gaining market feedback, and iterating based on what they learn to create a continuous conversation with customers. In essence, they are *discovering* their product at the same time they are *delivering* it. This has many results, but these are perhaps the two most important ones:

- The ability to learn, continuously and quickly, how well their products are meeting customer needs
- Raising customer expectations in terms of product quality and company response times to their concerns and feedback

What's more, this new way of working is not based on expensive technologies. The platforms and services that make this possible are available for free or nearly free to just about every startup team. This exposes incumbent businesses to a threat they haven't known before. Specifically, the barriers to entry—in almost every domain—have never been lower. Without the need to "manufacture" a physical product, anyone with access to the web can design, code, and deploy services to anyone else. Faced with these new threats, traditional "get it all figured out first" approaches are simply not workable. So what should product teams do?

It's time for a change.

---

1 Jon Jenkins, "Velocity 2011: Jon Jenkins, 'Velocity Culture,'" O'Reilly, June 20, 2011, YouTube video, 15:13, *https://oreil.ly/Yh7Co*; Joe McKendrick, "How Amazon Handles a New Software Deployment Every Second," ZDNet, March 24, 2105, *https://oreil.ly/zXFoo*; Werner Vogels, "The Story of Apollo - Amazon's Deployment Engine," All Things Distributed, November 12, 2014, *https://oreil.ly/HrMRs*.

Lean UX is the evolution of product design and team collaboration. It takes the best parts of the designer's toolkit, combines that with Agile software development and Lean Startup thinking, and makes all of this available to the entire product team. It allows teams to exploit this new reality to maximize learning, continuously discover the best path forward, and amplify the voice of the customer.

Lean UX is deeply collaborative and cross-functional because designers, product managers, and software engineers no longer have the luxury of working in isolation from each other. The days of the waterfall process are over. Work is continuous. We can't afford to wait on the work of others, nor can we keep others waiting on our work. Instead, we need daily, continuous engagement with our colleagues if we are going to be successful. This continuous engagement allows us to strip away heavy deliverables (and the time required to create them) in favor of techniques that build *shared understanding* with our teammates. Shared understanding allows our teams to make decisions faster and empowers us to engage in more strategic conversations. Yes, we still have the responsibility of getting the details right: crafting beautiful interface elements and elegant workflows, and thinking about all the little things that make a product design work, from accessibility to page load times, and from button labels to error messages. But by eliminating communication overhead, we have more time to focus on more fundamental activities like gathering insight that can affect strategic choices for our product.

Lean UX also lets us change the way we talk about design. Instead of talking about features and documents, we can talk about *what works*—the *outcomes* that we are trying to create. In this new reality, we have more access to market feedback than ever before. This allows us to reframe design conversations in terms of objective business, customer, and user goals. We can measure what works, learn, and adjust.

Lean UX is three things. It begins as a process change for designers and product teams. But it's much more than that. It's a culture change that lets us approach our work with humility; we acknowledge that our initial solutions will probably be wrong and use many sources of insight to continuously improve our thinking. Finally, it implies a set of organizational changes to the way we organize and manage software design and development teams to be more inclusive, collaborative, and transparent. We'll dig deeply into each of these aspects of Lean UX in the rest of the book.

Perhaps the best way to sum up this introduction, though, is this: *Lean UX is the way we need to work now.*

CHAPTER 2

Principles

Go that way. Really fast. If something gets in your way, turn!
Better Off Dead (1985)

At the heart of Lean UX, you'll find a core set of principles that govern the *design process*, *team culture*, and *team organization*. Treat these principles as a framework. Start with them to get your teams pointed in the right direction, and keep them in mind as you begin to implement the Lean UX processes we describe later in this book. It's really important to understand that Lean UX is *not* a set of rules. Instead, it's an approach that you adopt. Given the infinite variety of contexts that product teams work within and the different industries, companies, cultures, regulations, customers, and missions that designers serve, it's inevitable that you will need to adjust the processes we describe to make them work in your organization. The principles in this chapter will provide guidance to help you make those adjustments.

Ultimately, if you're able to apply principles, you'll find that you will change your team's culture. Some principles will have more impact than others, and some will be more difficult to act on. Regardless, each principle described here will help you to build a product design organization that is more collaborative, more cross-functional, and a better fit for today's agile reality.

The Foundations of Lean UX

Lean UX stands on a number of important foundations: it's a combination of a few different schools of thought. Understanding where it comes from will help you to apply the methods and find resources when you get stuck.

The first foundation of Lean UX is *user experience design*. Lean UX is, at its heart, a way of practicing user experience design. Drawing on roots in the fields of human factors and ergonomics as well as the human-centered design ideas that emerged in the 1950s with the work of industrial designers like Henry Dreyfuss, these methods and mindsets are known today as *user experience design* (or just UX), a term credited to Don Norman.[1] UX embraces a number of design fields, including interaction design, information architecture, graphic design, and many others. But the heart of UX practice is that it begins by identifying human needs—the needs of the users of the system.

In the past decade, we've seen the rise in popularity of *design thinking*. Design thinking emerged in the academy in the 1970s and 1980s and was popularized by the design firm IDEO in the early 2000s. It is a way of applying human-centered design methods to a wide range of problems. Tim Brown, CEO and president of IDEO, described design thinking as "innovation powered by...direct observation of what people want and need in their lives and what they like or dislike about the way particular products are made, packaged, marketed, sold, and supported."[2]

Brown continued: "[it's] a discipline that uses the designer's sensibility and methods to match people's needs with what is technologically feasible and what a viable business strategy can convert into customer value and market opportunity."

Design thinking is important for Lean UX because it takes the explicit position that every aspect of a business (or any other system) can be approached with design methods. It gives designers permission to work beyond their typical boundaries. It also encourages nondesigners to use design methods to solve the problems they face in their roles. So UX and its cousin, design thinking, form the critical first foundation that encourages teams to consider human needs, collaborate with nondesign roles, and approach product design from a holistic perspective.

The next foundation of Lean UX is *Agile software development*. Software developers have been using Agile methods for years to reduce their cycle times, build a cadence of continuous learning, and deliver customer value regularly. Although Agile methods can pose process challenges for designers (which we'll show you how to solve in Parts II and III), the core values of Agile are perfectly aligned with Lean UX. Lean UX applies the four core values of Agile development to product design:

---

1 Don Norman and Jakob Nielsen, "The Definition of User Experience," Nielsen Norman Group, accessed June 15, 2021, *https://oreil.ly/NxTKY*.

2 Tim Brown, "Design Thinking," *Harvard Business Review*, June 2008, *https://oreil.ly/zl9mr*.

1. Individuals and interactions over processes and tools.

   Lean UX favors collaboration and conversation over deliverables and rigid process. It engages the entire team to generate ideas from diverse points of view. It encourages the free and frequent exchange of ideas to allow the team to debate, decide, and move forward quickly.

2. Working software over comprehensive documentation.

   Every business problem has endless solutions, and each member of a team will have an opinion on which is best. The challenge is figuring out which solution is most viable. Sometimes, it's difficult or impossible to predict in advance which solution will work. By getting our ideas into the hands of customers (often through working software) sooner, the team can quickly assess solutions for market fit and viability.

3. Customer collaboration over contract negotiation.

   Collaborating with your teammates and customers builds a shared understanding of the problem space and the proposed solutions. It creates consensus behind decisions. The result? Faster iterations, real involvement in product making, and team investment in validated learning. It also lessens dependency on heavy documentation because everyone on the team has already participated in making the decisions. Collaboration creates alignment more effectively than written communication, argument, and elaborate defense.

4. Responding to change over following a plan.

   The assumption in Lean UX is that your initial product designs will be at least partially wrong, so the team's goal should be to find out what they got wrong as soon as possible. As soon as the team discovers what's working and what's not, they adjust their proposals and test again. This input from the market keeps teams agile, constantly nudging them in a "more right" direction.

The final foundation of Lean UX is Eric Ries's *Lean Startup* method. Lean Startup uses a feedback loop called "build-measure-learn" to minimize project risk and get teams building and learning quickly. Teams build *minimum viable products* (MVPs) and ship them quickly to begin the process of learning as early as possible.

As Eric puts it, "Lean Startup initially advocates the creation of rapid prototypes designed to test market assumptions and uses customer feedback to evolve them much faster than via more traditional software engineering practices."[3]

He continues: "Lean Startup processes reduce waste by increasing the frequency of contact with real customers, therefore testing and avoiding incorrect market assumptions as early as possible."

Lean UX is a direct application of this philosophy to the practice of product design.

Each design is a proposed business solution—a hypothesis. Your goal is to validate the proposed solution as efficiently as possible by using customer feedback. The smallest thing you can build to test each hypothesis is your MVP. The MVP doesn't need to be made of code: it can be an approximation of the end experience—it might not even be a product! You collect what you learn from your MVP and develop your ideas. Then you do it again.

So, What Is the Definition of Lean UX?

Here's how we define Lean UX:

- Lean UX is a design approach that brings the true nature of a product to light faster, in a collaborative, cross-functional, and user-centered way.
- Lean UX methods build a shared understanding of the user, their needs, our proposed solutions, and our definition of success.
- Lean UX prioritizes continuous learning to build evidence for team decisions and ensure ever-improving delivery of products, services, and value.

Principles

In the rest of this chapter, we'll lay out the principles behind Lean UX. As you explore this approach, keep these principles in mind. Think of your experience with Lean UX as a learning journey. Use these principles to keep yourself and your team on course.

We've organized these principles into three groups: principles to guide *team organization*, principles to guide *culture*, and principles to guide *process*.

---

3 Josh Seiden and Jeff Gothelf, "The 3 Foundations of Lean UX," O'Reilly Media, October 25, 2017, *https://oreil.ly/AFDOW*.

Principles to Guide Team Organization

Let's begin by taking a look at the Lean UX principles related to team organization:

- Cross-functional
- Small, dedicated, colocated
- Self-sufficient and empowered
- Problem-focused

Principle: Cross-functional

What is it? Cross-functional teams are made up of the various disciplines involved in creating your product. Software engineering, product management, interaction design, visual design, content strategy, marketing, quality assurance—these all make up a part of Lean UX teams. Lean UX demands a high level of collaboration among these disciplines. Their involvement must be continuous from day one of the project until the end of the engagement.

Why do it? Diverse teams create better solutions because each problem is seen from many different points of view. Creating diverse teams limits the need for gated, handoff-based ("waterfall") processes. Instead, teams can share information informally, which creates collaboration earlier in the process and drives greater team efficiency.

Principle: Small, dedicated, colocated

What is it? Keep your teams small—no more than 10 total core people. Dedicate them to one project and staff it all out of the same location.

Why do it? The benefit of small teams comes down to three words: communication, focus, and camaraderie. Smaller teams are easier to keep current on project status, changes, and new learning. Dedicating your team to one project keeps team members focused on the same priorities all the time and eliminates dependencies on other teams. Having the team all in one place allows relationships to grow between colleagues.

A Note About Colocation

In 2020, due to the COVID-19 pandemic, our industry was forced to learn a great deal about remote work. We'll talk about remote work in more depth later in the book, but for now, we want to comment on this principle and why we still advocate colocation. "Colocation" is about getting people together in the same physical space. We've learned in the last year that we can gather teams in a shared virtual space and create similar experiences. There are some benefits to this way of working (pajamas, cats, and less commuting time) and some drawbacks (pajamas, cats, and awkward digital collaboration tools). Overall, though, we believe that the core of what makes colocation powerful is the way it fosters shared understanding. It encourages teams to have casual, unplanned conversations and makes high-bandwidth multiperson collaborations so much easier. So though we've learned much about remote working, and though we've learned to make it work, we believe you lose something when you're not in a room together. So if you're working remotely, for whatever reason, try to do it in a way that limits handoffs, encourages informal collaboration, and seeks out the other subtle benefits of sitting in the same room with your colleagues.

Principle: Self-sufficient and empowered

What is it? Give your teams all the capabilities they need to operate without external dependencies. Ensure that they have the tools they need to create and release software. Give them permission to figure out how to solve the problems they face and to engage with users and customers through firsthand contact.

Why do it? Teams without external dependencies are free to optimize their process for maximum efficiency. They neither want for outside resources, nor do they want for external expertise. Teams that can create and release software themselves can move at a rapid pace and can maximize their learning. Finally, teams cannot learn from the market if they are not allowed to engage with the market. Teams must be able to interact with customers directly in order to get the feedback they need to create effective solutions.

Principle: Problem-focused

What is it? A problem-focused team is one that has been given a business or user problem to solve as opposed to a set of features to implement. In other words, this is a team that has been organized around an outcome.

Why do it? Assigning teams problems to solve shows trust in those teams. It allows them to come up with their own solutions and drives a deeper sense of pride and ownership in the solutions the team implements. It also changes what "done" looks like—instead of simply shipping a feature, teams that have the room to really solve problems will typically have to iterate until the problem is really solved.

Principles to Guide Culture

Culture and process are inextricable. Adopting Lean UX means adopting a culture of learning and curiosity. Here are the Lean UX principles that can help guide your culture toward that end state:

- Moving from doubt to certainty
- Outcomes, not output
- Removing waste
- Shared understanding
- No rock stars, gurus, or ninjas
- Permission to fail

Principle: Moving from doubt to certainty

What is it? Software development is complex and unpredictable. Because of this, Lean UX begins with the idea that everything is an assumption until we prove otherwise. As we work, we gain clarity. Thus, we are always moving from a position of doubt to one of certainty.

Why do it? Every project begins with a set of assumptions. Sometimes, these assumptions are easy to spot; sometimes we don't see them until it's too late. To eliminate the risk of investing a lot of time and effort in work that's based on bad assumptions, we begin by validating our assumptions. We adopt a mindset of *enthusiastic skepticism*. This means that we begin with doubt and proceed to validate what we know, as systematically and rigorously as we possibly can. In the process, our learning lets us become more certain about our positions as we pursue ongoing improvements to our work.

Principle: Outcomes over output

What is it? Features and services are *outputs*. The goals they are meant to achieve are *outcomes*. In Lean UX, teams are trying above all to create an outcome: *a measurable change in human behavior that creates value.* Lean UX measures progress in terms of explicitly defined outcomes.

Why do it? When we attempt to predict which features will achieve specific outcomes, we are mostly engaging in speculation. Although it's easier to manage the launch of specific feature sets, we often can't predict if a feature will be effective until it's in the market. By managing outcomes (and the progress made toward them), we gain insight into the efficacy of the features we are building. If a feature is not performing well, we can make an objective decision as to whether it should be kept, changed, or replaced.

Principle: Removing waste

What is it? One of the core tenets in Lean manufacturing is the removal of anything that doesn't lead to the ultimate goal. In Lean UX, the ultimate goal is improved outcomes; hence, anything that doesn't contribute to that is considered waste and should be removed from the team's process.

Why do it? Team resources are limited. The more a team can eliminate waste, the faster they can move. Teams want to work on the right challenges. They want to be effective. Thinking in terms of value creation and waste removal can help teams keep their laser focus where it belongs. Thinking about waste—and specifically *removing waste*—allows us to think critically about our design process. It encourages us to think about continuous improvement in the way that we work. But it's not just about the process. What's the ultimate waste? Making stuff that people don't want. Don't do that. Focus on the user and use your energy to deliver things that are valuable.

Principle: Shared understanding

What is it? Shared understanding is the collective knowledge that builds up over time as the team works together. It's a rich understanding of the space, the product, and the customers.

Why do it? Shared understanding is the currency of Lean UX. The more a team collectively understands what they're doing and why, the less they need to debate *what* happened and can quickly move to *how* to solve for the new learning. In addition, it reduces the team's dependencies on secondhand reports and detailed documents to continue its work. The more you can create a shared understanding of what users need, the more you are able to cut through ego, power plays, and self-referential design decisions.

Principle: No rock stars, gurus, or ninjas

What is it? Lean UX advocates a team-based mentality. Rock stars, gurus, ninjas—we use these labels to describe individual stars. Rather than focus on star performers, Lean UX seeks team cohesion and collaboration.

Why do it? Rock stars don't share—neither their ideas nor the spotlight. Team cohesion breaks down when you add individuals with large egos who are determined to stand out and be stars. When collaboration breaks down, you lose the environment you need to create the shared understanding required to move forward effectively.

Principle: Permission to fail

What is it? To find the best solution to business problems, Lean UX teams need to experiment with ideas. Most of these ideas will fail. *Permission to fail* means that the team has a safe environment in which to experiment. That applies to both the technical environment (they can push out ideas in a technically safe way) and the cultural environment (they won't be penalized for trying ideas that don't succeed).

Why do it? Permission to fail is the platform on which you build a culture of experimentation. Experimentation breeds creativity. Creativity, in turn, yields innovative solutions. When teams don't fear for their jobs if they get something wrong, they're more apt to take risks. It is from those risks that big ideas ultimately come.

The Virtues of Continuous Improvement

In a video called "Why You Need to Fail," CD Baby founder Derek Sivers describes the surprising results of a ceramics class.[4]

On the first day, the instructor announced to his class that the students would be divided into two groups. Half of the students would only need to make one clay pot each during the semester. Their grades would depend on the perfection of that solitary pot. The other half of the class would be graded simply by the weight of the pots they made during the semester. If they made 50 pounds of pots or more, they'd get an A. Forty pounds would earn a B; 30 pounds, a C; and so on. What they actually made was irrelevant. The instructor said he wouldn't even look at their pots. He would simply bring his bathroom scale to the final day of class and weigh the students' work.

At the end of the semester, an interesting thing had occurred. Outside observers of the class noted that the highest-quality pots had been made by the "quantity group." They had spent the entire semester working as quickly as they could to make pots. Sometimes they succeeded, and sometimes they failed. With each iteration, each experiment, they learned. From that learning, they became better able to achieve the end goal: making high-quality clay pots.

By contrast, the group that made one object didn't have the benefit of those failed iterations and didn't learn quickly enough to perform at the same level as the "quantity group." They had spent their semester theorizing about what would make a "grade-A" clay pot but didn't have the experience to execute that grandiose vision.

---

4 Derek Sivers, "Why You Need to Fail - by Derek Sivers," February 15, 2011, YouTube video, 14:54, *https://oreil.ly/oZHQe*.

Principles to Guide Process

Now that we have a sense of the broader organizational and cultural principles, let's take a tactical look at how teams need to change the way they're working:

- Don't do the same thing faster.
- Beware of phases.
- Iteration is the key to agility.
- Work in small batches to mitigate risk.
- Embrace continuous discovery.
- Get out of the building.
- Externalize your work.
- Make over analysis.
- Get out of the deliverables business.

Principle: don't do the same thing faster

What is it? When teams adopt Agile, the first attempts often involve doing the same things they've always done, just faster. This never works out well. You can't do eight weeks of research in two weeks. Don't even try. Instead, you need to behave in a new way. You need to reconceptualize the work.

Why do it? The goal of Agile isn't to work fast. It's not to work in two-week sprints. The goal isn't to follow all the rules. The goal is to work in a way that's appropriate to the medium of software and, in doing so, to make better products and services that deliver more value. So Agile methods give us an opportunity to rethink the way we work, the way we collaborate, the way we deliver value. Sometimes, we can simply fit old processes into Agile rhythms. Sometimes, we can't. When that happens, don't force the methods—rethink them!

Principle: beware of phases

What is it? Any time you have a research phase, a design phase, a development phase, a testing phase, a (God forbid) hardening phase, really, an *anything-phase*, it should serve as a warning sign that something's wrong. Agile teams should be doing all of these things continuously, in every sprint. You should be researching continuously. Designing continuously. Building continuously. Testing....You get the point.

Why do we do it? Agile work is based on a fundamental idea: inspect and adapt. You want to have finished work that you can inspect on a frequent, regular basis. Phases—whether they're research phases, design phases, build phases, whatever—don't result in finished work. They result in finished *process steps*. To get to finished work, you need to move from phased work to continuous work.

Principle: iteration is the key to agility

What is it? When you're breaking work into small batches, don't settle for incremental slices. Instead, take an iterative approach. Expect to design and test your work—often the same work—multiple times until you get it right.

Why do it? Many Agile teams mix up incremental approaches (slicing a big feature into small parts and delivering it over several sprints) with iterative approaches (working on a feature over and over in order to improve it). In part, this is because we value working in small batches, and both approaches are indeed small-batch approaches. Iteration, though, is a commitment to redoing your work until you get it right, until it solves the problem you're trying to solve, until it meets user needs (not simply meets the functional spec), until it delivers the *outcome* that you're trying to create. Iteration is also the key to ending one of the most common frustrations that UX designers experience in the Agile world: the feeling that *we never get enough time to get it right*. By working on a feature until it's right, teams have a chance to deliver great work that they are proud of, that satisfies the user, and that solves the problem the business sets out to solve.

Principle: work in small batches to mitigate risk

What is it? Another fundamental from Lean manufacturing is the practice of dividing work into small units or *batches*. Lean manufacturing uses this notion to keep inventory low and quality high. Translated to Lean UX, this means creating only the design that is necessary to move the team forward and avoiding a big "inventory" of untested and unimplemented design ideas.

Why do it? Every project begins with assumptions. Large-batch design begins with those untested assumptions and creates a lot of design work on top of them. This means that if we find out that a foundational assumption is wrong, we must throw away a lot of work. By working in smaller batches, we can design and validate our decisions as we go, which reduces the risk of wasted work.

Principle: embrace continuous discovery

What is it? Continuous discovery is the ongoing process of engaging the customer during the design and development process. This is done through regularly scheduled activities, using both quantitative and qualitative methods. The goal is to understand both *what* the user is doing with your products and *why* they are doing it. So you do research on a frequent basis and a regular rhythm. Research involves the entire team.

Why do it? Regular customer conversations provide frequent opportunities for validating new product ideas. Bringing the entire team into the research cycle develops empathy for users and the problems they face. You create shared understanding. Finally, as the team learns together, you reduce the need for future debrief conversations and documentation.

Principle: get out of the building

What is it? This phrase, made popular by Steve Blank, Stanford professor, entrepreneur, and author, refers to the practice of what UX people know simply as "user research." In the Lean manufacturing world, you'll hear a similar idea expressed as "go and see."

What all of these communities have codiscovered is the idea that you won't find the truth about your users in a conference room. You have to go to where they are, observe what they're doing, and actually engage with them in order to understand what they're doing, what they're trying to do, and *why* they're trying to do it.

Lean UX aligns with this prescription: give potential customers a chance to provide feedback on your ideas sooner than you would have in the past. Much sooner. Test your ideas with a strong dose of reality while they're still young. Better to find out that your ideas are missing the mark before you've spent time and resources building a product that no one wants.

Why do it? Ultimately, the success or failure of your product isn't the team's decision—it's the customer's. They will need to click that "Buy Now" button you designed. The sooner you give them a voice, the sooner you'll learn whether you've got an idea that works.

Principle: externalize your work

What is it? Externalizing means getting your work out of your head and out of your computer and into public view. Teams use whiteboards, virtual shared spaces, foam-core boards, artifact walls, printouts, and sticky notes to expose their work in progress to their teammates, colleagues, and customers.

Why do it? Externalizing work allows everyone to see where the team stands. It creates a passive, ambient flow of information across the team. It inspires new ideas that build off the ones that have already been shared. It allows all the members of the team—even the quiet ones—to participate in information-sharing activities. Their sticky notes or whiteboard sketches are equally as loud as the most prominent person on the team.

Principle: make over analysis

What is it? Lean UX values making over analysis. There is more value in creating the first version of an idea than spending half a day debating its merits in a conference room.

Why do it? The answer to most difficult questions the team will face will not be answered in a conference room; it's the customers in the field who will answer them. To get those answers, you need to make the ideas concrete—you need to make something for people to respond to. Debating ideas without market-based data is waste. Instead of analyzing potential scenarios, make something and get out of the building with it.

Principle: get out of the deliverables business

What is it? Lean UX shifts the focus of the design process away from the documents the team is creating. Instead, it focuses on the outcomes the team is achieving. With increased cross-functional collaboration, stakeholder conversation becomes less about what artifact is being created and more about which outcome is being achieved.

Why do it? Documents don't solve customer problems—good products do. The team's focus should be on learning which features have the biggest impact on its customers. The artifacts the team uses to gain and communicate that knowledge are irrelevant. All that matters is the quality of the product, as measured by the market's reaction to it.

Wrapping Up

This chapter put forward a set of foundational principles for Lean UX. These are the core attributes that any Lean UX team should strive to embody. As you begin to form your practice, we encourage you to use these principles to define your team's makeup, location, goals, and practices.

CHAPTER 3

Outcomes

Traditionally, software projects are framed by requirements and deliverables. Teams are given requirements and are expected to create deliverables. These deliverables will describe systems, features, and technology that will satisfy those requirements. In many cases, requirements arrive without strategic context. Why are we doing this? For whom? What does success look like?

Lean UX radically shifts the way we frame our work by introducing back the strategic context for our feature and design choices and, more important, how we—the entire team, not just the design department—define success. Our goal is not to create a deliverable or a feature: it's to positively affect customer behavior or change in the world—to create an outcome.

What Business Are We In?

Lean UX means *getting out of the deliverables business*. We're in the business of creating outcomes. We must focus less on the stuff we make—the documentation and mock-ups and prototypes, the features and pages and buttons—and more on generating results. To do that, we focus on only making things that generate the outcomes that we want.

Why focus on outcomes instead of features and deliverables? It's because we've learned that it's hard—and in many cases impossible—to predict whether the features we design and build will create the value we want to create. *Will this button encourage people to purchase? Will this feature create more engagement? Will people use this feature in ways we didn't predict? Will we successfully shift the way people interact with our service?* So, rather than focus on the features, it's better to focus on the value we're trying to create and keep testing solutions until we find one that delivers the value—the outcome—that we desire.

This shift in emphasis applies both to the things that designers make as part of their process—documents, mock-ups, wireframes, specifications, prototypes— and to the way we frame our work. What is the result that our clients or stakeholders want? Sure, they may be asking us to create a website or an app. They may be asking for a new page, a new flow, some new copy. But they're asking that for a reason—and part of our job is to understand and articulate that reason. We'll dig into *how* to do that in the next part of the book. For now, though, we want to equip you with a little bit of language to help you reframe your work away from deliverables and toward results—in other words, to move from *outputs* to *outcomes*.

A Story About Outcomes

Imagine a small team working at an agency. Jono, Nicole, Alex, and Amanda are meeting with a new client for the first time. The client has hired the agency to design, build, and launch a new website that they are committed to launching later in the year.

The client team has prepared for this first meeting. They've prepared and sent a detailed list of requirements that the website must meet. The feature list is ambitious and, for the agency team, more than a little scary. The agency team has done their homework too. They've reviewed the requirements list, and they have a set of questions ready for the client.

After some introductions and pleasantries, Nicole cuts to the chase. She says, "So we've had a chance to review the requirements list, and there's a lot here. One thing that would help us would be to step away from the requirements for a moment and just talk about the purpose of the site and service. Can you tell us why this service is important for your business?"

"Sure," says Cecily, the CEO of the small company that has hired the agency. "We currently operate a very high-end adventure-travel and event-planning service for perhaps 50 clients a year. It's a very high-touch service. We'd like to launch an online version of our service so that we can serve thousands of clients each year. We know the demand is there, but the economics require a lower-touch approach, and that's what this website will provide."

"That's great," says Nicole. Jono goes to the whiteboard and writes *Impact: a successful low-touch service that allows us to serve thousands of clients each year.*

Nicole continues: "And when this service is live, what will customers be able to do that they can't do today?"

"Well," says Cecily, pausing for a moment. "That's a good question. Our current service is a specialized event-planning service for bespoke events in exotic locations. We do all of the planning ourselves. In our new service, we'd like event hosts who don't require our travel expertise to be able to find event planners to work with that fit their budgets and their needs."

"Awesome," says Jono, who writes on the board *Outcome: event hosts will meet qualified event planners for domestic and local events.*

Cecily looks at the board, a bit puzzled. She says, "That's all obvious stuff. Why does this help you?"

Nicole explains, "Well, the feature list in your requirements document is very ambitious." This is Nicole's polite way of explaining that the list is unreasonably long and veers frequently into speculation. She continues: "Since your deadline is pretty short, we're going to need to filter the list and decide what to build first and what features can wait until later. Understanding the outcome our users want will help us prioritize the feature list so that we can focus on things that help customers meet each other, find projects, and bid on them together. Anything that doesn't create that outcome will get deprioritized."

Unpacking the Story: Output, Outcomes, Impact

Now, the story above is fiction, but it's based on countless real kickoff meetings, and it illustrates one of the key ideas in Lean UX: Lean UX is about focusing on outcomes.

Let's look at the story in a little more detail and talk a bit about the framework behind Nicole and Jono's process.

First, the client arrived with a long list of requirements—these requirements described the website and the features of the site that they wanted the agency to design and build. These are the things that they wanted the agency to make: *the output.*

The agency team knew that the list of features was too long—it would take a long time to build everything in the requirements document—and, worse, they suspected that many of the features in that list wouldn't be useful to end users *or* to the client. So the agency team was looking to get beyond the feature list.

When Nicole asked about the *impact* that the client was seeking, she was going to the big picture. If the CEO wanted to keep her job, what would she need to deliver to the board? We use the word "impact" to describe the highest-level targets that a business sets. These tend to be things like revenue, profit, customer loyalty. But they can also be big, strategic objectives, like Cecily's goal to grow from a boutique provider of services into an organization with broader reach.

The problem with big targets—impact-level targets—is that there are so many ways to pursue them, and so many factors that contribute to them, that it can be difficult to know how to break down the work and how to measure progress toward that target. To address that, we use an intermediate target, called an "outcome." In this case, the team captured the most important intermediate target they would be working toward, which was the outcome: *To allow qualified professionals to meet one another and create collaborative project bids.*

So, while outputs are things we make, like websites and features, outcomes are things that people do. In fact, that's the key to our definition of outcomes. We define an outcome as *"a change in human behavior that creates value."*[1] When we use this definition of outcome, we are using an inherently human-centered idea to define success. When we move away from outputs—the stuff we make—and toward outcomes, we're choosing to put humans and their needs at the center of what we do.

The Logic Model

We've drawn our language (outputs, outcomes, impact) from a model called the logic model, first described in 2004 by the W. K. Kellogg Foundation. This model has proven popular in the nonprofit world. The goal of the model was to help people running complex projects evaluate the efficacy of those programs. When granters give money for a program, they typically have an impact in mind. How can they evaluate whether their grant money is being well spent? The logic model framework was developed to help program evaluators answer this question. The model is usually visualized as shown in Figure 3-1.

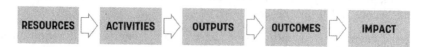

Figure 3-1. *The logic model*

In our work with teams, we've discovered that this model can be really useful to Agile teams. We've adapted it a bit for our more limited context. But if you're interested in learning more, we encourage you to go to the source and read more about program evaluation at the Kellogg Foundation site.

---

1 To learn more about outcomes, see Josh's book *Outcomes Over Output: Why Customer Behavior Is the Key Metric for Business Success* (Sense & Respond Press, 2019), *https://oreil.ly/7O2xZ*.

A deeper look at an outcome

Let's take a closer look at the outcome in our story. First, we said that an outcome is *a change in behavior*. What do we mean by that? In our story, our outcome was: *meet qualified professionals and create collaborative project bids*. This project—if it's successful—will encourage a behavior: professionals will meet one another online in order to create project bids together. This might be a new behavior—something that these professionals can't do today—or it might simply be a better way to do something that they do today. Either way, we consider that a *behavior change*.

And what about the *creates value* part of our definition? Well, if our work is successful, these professionals will be able to do this new thing, and they'll get value from being able to do it. So, then, we've satisfied both parts of our definition. Professionals will be able to *do this new thing*, and *they'll get value from doing it*.

Now, what's interesting here is that this new behavior also creates value for the organization. They benefit from this new customer behavior, because when they satisfy their customer, the customer pays them for the service, is more likely to pay them again in the future, and is also more likely to recommend the service to others. If you're reading closely, you'll notice that these are also customer behaviors—customers pay for service, they return for more service, they recommend the service. All of these are outcomes, too, but these outcomes don't necessarily benefit the user. Instead, these outcomes benefit the organization.

That's an important thing to pay attention to when we work with outcomes: *who is getting value from the behavior in question?* When a professional can do business more easily, they are getting that value. When the customer pays for this outcome, the organization is getting the value. In other words, value depends on your point of view. We'll talk about this in more detail in Chapter 8. For now, just remember that every outcome comes with a point of view baked in, and it's important to understand whose point of view we're thinking about. (See Figure 3-2.)

Let's look at a system like Facebook for an example of point of view. When an end user logs on to Facebook, they get value from reading and posting to the timeline. Advertisers get value when timeline users see and interact with ads. And Facebook gets value when users spend more time on the site and advertisers pay them for access to these people. If you want your system to work, you need to create a set of aligned outcomes—you need to understand the ways that different users get value and then deliver that value to them in a way that *also* creates value for your organization.

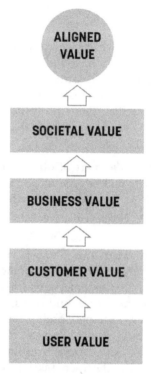

Figure 3-2. *Aligned value*

The Facebook example brings up another point of view here, which relates to the value the system creates for people who don't directly use the system. Facebook's impact on society is—well, let's call it *controversial*. In terms of our model, they have created a way to deliver value to users, advertisers, and themselves, but at what cost to society? A robust and ethical framework for aligning value has to take into account the needs of a broad range of stakeholders—both those who directly interact with the system and those who are indirectly impacted.[2]

This brings us to a final point here: none of the systems that we work on can be described with a single outcome statement. They are all systems of interrelated outcomes. What's more, all of these related outcomes combine to create the high-level impact (or impacts) that we seek. This can make working with out-

---

2 For a good summary of the issues here, see Oz Lubling's article "The Blurry Line between Empowerment and Exploitation in UX," Culture Clash, February 4, 2021, *https://oreil.ly/BDi2z*.

comes tricky—a typical system is composed of many people performing many behaviors. It's easy to quickly get overwhelmed. What behaviors are important? Which ones should we focus on? In coming chapters, we'll share some techniques for discovering, understanding, and mapping these related outcomes and for navigating through this complexity to find the key outcomes to focus on.

Outcomes, Iteration, and Validation

When you shift the focus of your work from outputs to outcomes, it creates huge changes in the way you organize your work. One of the big things that changes is the finish line: how do you know when you're done?

In the software world, we typically use requirements, specifications, and acceptance criteria to tell us when work is done. Is the software running? Does it meet the specs? Comply with requirements? Meet the acceptance criteria? Does it meet what Scrum calls the "definition of done"? These methods are good in that they can define the finish line very precisely, but they almost always ask us to evaluate the *output* of our work. What if we don't want to stop there? What if we want to measure the *outcomes* that we've created?

It turns out that, in this case, we can't stop working on a thing when we've finished making it. To measure outcomes, we actually need to put that thing in the world and observe how (or if) it changes people's behaviors. In other words, while we have to complete the output, that's not enough. We have to *validate it*.

The process of validating our output is inherently iterative. Most of the time, teams don't get everything right on their first attempt. Typically, our first attempt may get some of the outcome we seek but usually not all of it. When we focus on outcomes, we see the opportunity for improvement, and we keep working on that thing until it delivers the outcomes that we set out to deliver. This is the process that Lean Startup calls the *build-measure-learn loop* and what the Agile community calls *inspect and adapt*. Whatever you call these loops, they describe an iterative approach. An approach that means the end of one-and-done. An approach that means we iterate until we achieve the outcome.

PROCESS

About Part II

In the previous part, we looked at the ideas behind Lean UX—the principles that drive the work. In this section, we'll get very practical and describe in detail the process of doing Lean UX.

We've organized this section around a new tool that we've been using for the last few years: the Lean UX Canvas. The Lean UX Canvas is a way to orchestrate your Lean UX process. It offers a single-page "at-a-glance" way of framing your work on a feature, an epic or initiative, or even an entire product.

This single-page tool collects all of the key tools, methods, processes, and techniques of Lean UX into a single document with a unified structure. It's a tool that you can use to get from the earliest part of the design process—your initial problem framing—through design, prototyping, and research.

Although you don't *have* to use the canvas to do Lean UX, we've found that the canvas is a great way to explain the process, so we've chosen to present the Lean UX process to you by using the canvas.

The Lean UX Canvas

Chapter 4, "The Lean UX Canvas", provides an overview of the Lean UX Canvas. You'll learn why Lean UX is skeptical of requirements, why it embraces assumptions instead, and how the Lean UX Canvas is a vehicle that you can use to capture and test your assumptions. This chapter also introduces some ideas about facilitating the process of working with the canvas.

Chapter 5, "Box 1: Business Problem", covers the technique you'll use to define the problem you and your team are trying to solve from the business's POV.

Chapter 6, "Box 2: Business Outcomes", covers how you define success for your project. This box is all about understanding what outcomes you're trying to achieve for your business, organization, or clients.

Chapter 7, "Box 3: Users", covers the section of the canvas that defines your users (and customers). This section describes the proto-persona technique and how to use it.

Chapter 8, "Box 4: User Outcomes and Benefits", is all about user goals. What are your users (and customers) trying to do? What will define success for them?

Chapter 9, "Box 5: Solutions", is where we begin to define what we'll be making (or doing) in order to solve the problems we've defined.

Chapter 10, "Box 6: Hypotheses", Chapter 11, "Box 7: What's the Most Important Thing We Need to Learn First?", and Chapter 12, "Box 8: MVPs and Experiments", cover the bottom third of the canvas, which drives the conversation to find out if we're right about everything else in the canvas.

Let's dig into each box and see exactly how each part of this conversation plays out, how to facilitate it successfully, and what to watch out for in each box as you go through the exercises and declare your assumptions.

The Lean UX Canvas

Assumptions Are the New Requirements

If you work in an industry where things are relatively predictable, where there is low risk and high certainty in what the company is making, what it takes to make your product, what it looks like when it's done, and what your customers will do with it once they have it, you can comfortably work with a set of rigid, predetermined requirements. In a world with this manufacturing-era mentality, big design up front is the norm, and any variability in the production of your product is seen not as an agile response to a changing marketplace but rather as an expensive deviation from the plan. This way of thinking about requirements was adopted in the early days of the software industry, was the dominant model for decades, and continues to permeate many teams' ways of working even to this day.

Requirements assume we know exactly what we need to build. Ideally, they come from engineering rigor. But in software, they usually don't have the rigor behind them. Still, they are taken at face value based on their author's credibility or organizational title. In many cases, that blind faith is augmented with the phrase "well, it worked before." Individuals or teams who question the absoluteness of the requirements they've received are perceived as troublemakers and treated as scapegoats when projects end up missing deadlines, exceeding scope, or both. In organizations still leaning heavily on them as a way to tell teams what to do, requirements often simply mean, as our friend Jeff Patton likes to say, "Shut up."

But today's software-based businesses operate in a reality devoid of consistency, predictability, stability, and certainty. Saying with authority that a specific combination of code, copy, and design will achieve a desired business outcome and will be delivered completely by an explicit deadline is not just risky; in most cases it's a lie. Software development is complex and unpredictable. The pace of change is incredibly fast. Not only can companies ship features to production continuously at unprecedented speeds, but consumer behaviors are changing just as quickly. As soon as you've settled on a feature set, design approach, and specific user experience, your audience begins to evolve into new mental models based on their experiences with other online services.

The good news is that we don't have to rely on requirements. The industry has developed new ways to work that allow us to move away from rigid requirements. When we wrote the first edition of this book, Amazon was shipping code to production every 11.6 seconds. Today they've decreased their time to market to one second.[1] That's right: every second some Amazon customer somewhere in their ecosystem experiences a change to the way the product works. Sixty times per minute, Amazon has an opportunity to learn how well they're meeting the needs of their customers. Sixty times per minute, they have an opportunity to respond to what they're learning. Sixty times per minute, they have an opportunity to make their user experience better. With this capability, the very idea of a rigid requirement is, at best, anachronistic. At worst, it's an impediment that prevents teams from doing their best work. We'll grant that Amazon is at the extreme end of this, but they serve as inspiration and a clear target for what is possible. If we can ship, sense, and respond to this quickly, then assuming that we know exactly how to best deliver value is a level of arrogance and risk your organization cannot afford.

There are other reasons to avoid requirements. Software is hard. Even seasoned software engineers will tell you that just because something *seems* simple to build doesn't mean it actually will *be* simple to build. Oftentimes, as we set out to deliver a specific user experience, we learn that in order to do so we'll need to develop more code than we anticipated. The code we thought would be simple turns out to have complex dependencies or has legacy constraints or runs into unplanned obstacles, and we end up having to spend extra time figuring out how to work around these problems. This, too, flies in the face of rigid, deadline-based requirements.

And, of course, it's not just code that is complex and unpredictable. Humans are complex and unpredictable too. Their innate motivations, personalities, expectations, cultural norms, and habits all fly in the face of what we believe will be an ideal software service for them to use. We put so much faith in what we think will be "easy to use" or "intuitive," only to find that our target

---

1 Vogels, "The Story of Apollo - Amazon's Deployment Engine."

audience goes out of their way to avoid the simplifications we believe we made for them. Why do they do this? Any variety of factors (which we could learn about through customer interviews and research) could lead to these unexpected behaviors, but they all have the same net result: they prove our requirements wrong.

So what should we do? We need to recognize that most requirements are simply *assumptions* expressed with authority. If we remove the authority, overconfidence, and arrogance from the conversation, we're left with someone's best guess about how to best achieve a user goal or solve a business problem. We are makers of digital products, so humbly admitting that these are indeed our best guesses or assumptions immediately and explicitly creates the space for product discovery and Lean UX to take place. If we understand as a team that the work we're undertaking is risky *exactly because* we can't predict human behavior, we know that part of our work will have to include experimentation, research, and rework. We reduce our attachment to the ideas and create a team culture that is more willing to adjust course—even to stop working on an idea that continues to prove unviable.

So how do we build a conversation that encourages ideas from the whole team but qualifies those ideas as a series of assumptions? In earlier versions of this book we shared a series of assumptions declaration exercises. These processes have helped readers and practitioners express their ideas in a new way, as *testable assumptions*. Over the years, we've consolidated these assumptions declaration exercises, as well as the steps you'll need to test your assumptions, into one comprehensive facilitation tool we call the Lean UX Canvas.

The Lean UX Canvas

The Lean UX Canvas (Figure 4-1) brings together a series of exercises that allow teams to declare their assumptions about an initiative. It's designed to facilitate conversations within the team but also with stakeholders, clients, and other colleagues. Remember that in Lean UX we're trying to build shared understanding, and to do that (especially when we're trying to move away from requirements), we need a consistent shared vocabulary that allows stakeholders and individual contributors alike to share their ideas and create clarity.

If you've done some Lean UX work in the past, you'll recognize most of these activities. If you've done design work before, you'll recognize the importance of all of the topics on the canvas and how important it is to have conversations about these topics at the start of a project. Our experience using this canvas is that the structure of the canvas helps ensure all these conversations take place, that the conversations include a diverse set of viewpoints, and that, when you're done, the extended team has built shared understanding and the path forward is clear.

Lean UX Canvas (v2)

Title of initiative:

Date:

Iteration:

Business Problem

What problem does the business have that you are trying to solve?

(Hint: Consider your current offerings and how they deliver value, changes in the market, delivery channels, competitive threats and customer behavior.)

1

Users

What types (i.e., personas) of users and customers should you focus on first?

(Hint: Who buys your product or service? Who uses it? Who configures it? Etc)

3

Hypotheses

Combine the assumptions from 2, 3, 4 & 5 into the following hypothesis statement:
"We believe that [business outcome] will be achieved if [user] attains [benefit] with [feature]."

(Hint: Each hypothesis should focus on one feature only.)

6

Solutions

What can we make that will solve our business problem and meet the needs of our customers at the same time? List product, feature, or enhancement ideas here.

5

What's the most important thing we need to learn first?

For each hypothesis from Box 6, identify its riskiest assumptions. Then determine the riskiest one right now. This is the assumption that will cause the entire idea to fail if it's wrong.

(Hint: In the early stages of a hypothesis focus on risks to value rather than feasibility.)

7

Business Outcomes

How will you know you solved the business problem? What will you measure?

(Hint: What will people/users be doing differently if your solutions work? Consider metrics that indicate customer success like average order value, time on site, and retention rate.)

2

User Outcomes & Benefits

Why would your users seek out your product or service? What benefit would they gain from using it? What behavior change can we observe that tells us they've achieved their goal?

(Hint: Save money, get a promotion, spend more time with family)

4

What's the least amount of work we need to do to learn the next most important thing?

Design experiments to learn as fast as you can whether your riskiest assumption is true or false.

8

(cc) BY-NC-SA Download this canvas: www.jeffgothelf.com/blog/leanuxcanvas-v2

Figure 4-1. *The Lean UX Canvas (https://www.jeffgothelf.com/blog/leanuxcanvas-v2)*

The canvas was designed to guide the conversation from the current state of your product or system—or what Mike Rother called *the current condition* ("NOW" in Figure 4-2) in his book *The Toyota Kata*[2]—to its desired future state or *target condition* ("LATER" in Figure 4-2).

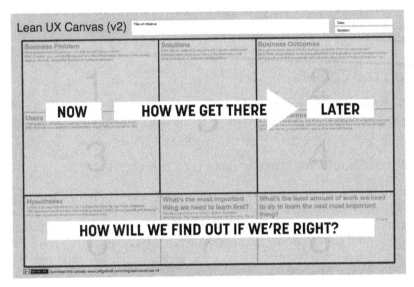

Figure 4-2. *The key areas of the Lean UX Canvas*

Another Canvas?

Another canvas? Fair question. Ever since Alex Osterwalder and the team at Strategyzer gifted the world the Business Model Canvas, we've been enamored and ultimately inundated with canvases. If you don't publish a canvas, are you really even a thought leader? Again, fair question. But canvases are useful and can serve as the centerpiece of a balanced, inclusive team collaboration. If used correctly, canvases:

- Consolidate a series of activities into a sequential process designed to drive a narrative.
- Help in complex environments. They help us create a single visual model to represent key elements of that complexity.
- Serve as an easy-to-follow facilitation tool for teams interested in having a specific kind of conversation.

---

2 Mike Rother, *The Toyota Kata: Managing People for Improvement, Adaptiveness, and Superior Results* (McGraw-Hill Education, 2009).

- Level the playing field for team members less apt to offer their ideas in a standard brainstorming session.
- Create a shared language for the team to use.
- Successfully frame the job to be done by the team.
- Communicate the challenge or work the team is undertaking broadly beyond the team.

Using the Canvas

In the coming chapters, we'll describe each section of the canvas in detail. Before we do that, however, we want to answer some general questions that come up whenever we teach teams about the canvas.

So When Should We Use the Lean UX Canvas?

We think that the canvas is a great way to start an initiative. Whether you're working on a new feature, a major initiative, or a new product, the canvas is a great structure to use for your kickoff meeting. As you get comfortable with the tool, you'll start to develop a sense of when a piece of work is too small for the canvas. Generally, we think it's a good idea to use it any time you're planning a big chunk of work.

Is the Lean UX Canvas Best Suited for Early-Stage Ideas or for Sustaining Innovation?

The canvas actually works well for both types of work. The key question is this: are you facing important unknowns, uncertainty, or complexity? That's where the Lean UX Canvas—and, really, Lean UX in general—can help. In early-stage work, the unknowns tend to be existential in nature: is there a need for this product or service? Will people use our solution? Can we build a business by solving this problem? In sustaining innovation, the questions tend to be smaller, but that doesn't mean that the answers are any clearer. In both of these situations, the Lean UX Canvas can help.

Who Should Work on the Canvas?

One of the values of the canvas is the way that working through it creates shared understanding on your team. It encourages the team and stakeholders to do the product discovery work that makes for successful products. So we believe that all team members should participate in the work on the canvas. We also think that stakeholders and clients should participate as much as possible, especially during the parts of the work to elaborate the business problem statement and business goals.

How Long Should We Expect to Spend on a Lean UX Canvas?

It's hard to get through the whole thing in less than a half-day session. Because the canvas makes a great kickoff activity, think about how much time you normally spend kicking off projects. Is that a two-day exercise? A full week? Some teams will work through the canvas that way, especially if you can all be together in the same room. Other teams will choose to hold a series of meetings over the course of a couple of weeks. In general, the bigger and more important the project, the longer it will take. Don't get stuck in analysis paralysis. When you don't know something, put it in the parking lot and move on. After all, the *whole point* of the canvas is to collect the things that you don't know so that you can start learning about them quickly.

Do We Have to Use the Canvas to Do Lean UX?

Absolutely not. Each part of the canvas contains a useful part of the Lean UX process. As you're working on any initiative, you're going to want to think about and answer the questions implied by each of the boxes on the canvas. That said, you can absolutely use each box on the canvas as a standalone technique. Are you unclear about your users? Go to Box 3, read about protopersonas, and use these ideas with your team to get clarity. Are you unclear about the best solution to a problem? Flip to the section of this book on Box 5 and take your team through that process.

If you decide to use the canvas as a whole, remember that it's a flexible tool. Use the exercises that work best for you, taking into account your context and the ways that work for your team. Expand the number of activities as your team grows more comfortable with the nature of this work. Ultimately, we want to ensure the customer is front and center in all of your conversations. The Lean UX Canvas is a strong starting point for ensuring that happens.

Facilitating Each Section

In the chapters to come, we'll share instructions for exercises that we like to use to complete the canvas. Here, we'd like to note some general patterns.

Be inclusive

We want the whole team to participate in completing the canvas.[3] This means that your facilitation needs to account for different participation styles, as well as the different levels of power and authority in the room.

---

3 The idea of "the whole team" will vary based on your context, so feel free to adapt this advice based on the size of your group and the roles of the people in the room.

To address that, we like to use a variant of the *1-2-4-All* pattern.[4] This is a structured way of eliciting participation from a group. Here's how it works:

- You start by asking people to work individually (the "1"), usually silently, either by writing ideas or drawing something by themselves. You generally want to set an aggressive time limit on this period (usually five minutes) to force people to get their ideas out and to avoid spending a lot of time editing and refining. After this period of solo work, ask folks to share back with their table or their subgroup. If people have been working with Post-its, it can make sense to ask people to bring them to a wall and post them there. Optionally, you can offer discussion during this period. You can also ask people to do some affinity mapping at this point.
- Then, you ask people to work in pairs (the "2") to elaborate or develop an idea. Paired work takes more time than solo work, so give the pairs more time than you allowed for solo work. Again, following this period of paired work, you have the pairs present their work to their table or subgroup room, and you may have more discussion at this point.
- Next, you ask each table or subgroup to develop their work into a single presentation. (This is the "4" portion of the pattern.)
- Finally (if you're trying to produce one final idea), you ask the whole group to develop a single idea. (This is the "All" portion of the pattern.)

1-2-4-All is effective because it solicits input from everyone in the room, allows for both solo and collaborative working styles, and, finally, allows the group to come together. You'll want to adapt this pattern to the specific exercise but keep it in mind as you plan group work.

Remote versus in-person

All of these exercises can be done as in-person workshops or remotely, with videoconferencing software and shared whiteboard tools. If you're working remotely, remember to break up your sessions to allow people to stand up and avoid Zoom fatigue. Also, remember that not everyone is familiar with online whiteboard tools, so allow some time to bring less experienced participants up to speed. (Sometimes you can use an icebreaker exercise that helps people learn the tool.) We've created Lean UX Canvas templates (*http://www.leanux book.com/links*) that you can use.

---

4 This is one of the patterns in the very useful Liberating Structures collection. See "1-2-4-All," Liberating Structures, accessed June 16, 2021, *https://oreil.ly/12vgk*.

Wrapping Up

In the coming chapters in this section, we'll describe each section of the canvas in detail.

CHAPTER 5

Box 1: Business Problem

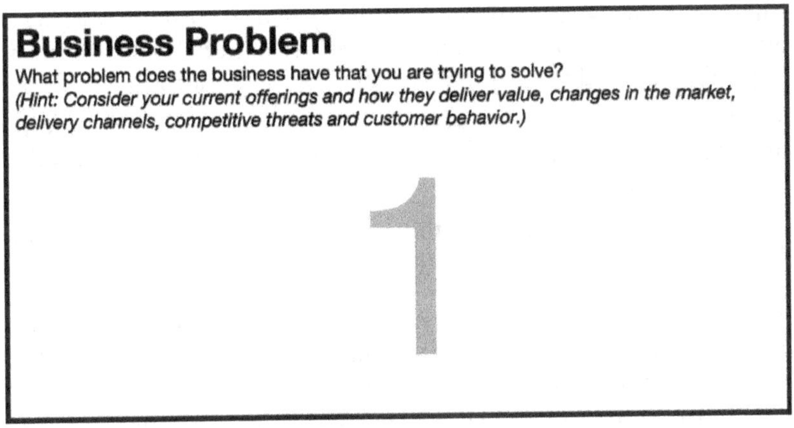

Business Problem
What problem does the business have that you are trying to solve?
(Hint: Consider your current offerings and how they deliver value, changes in the market, delivery channels, competitive threats and customer behavior.)

1

Figure 5-1. *Box 1 of the Lean UX Canvas: Business Problem*

For Lean UX to be successful, teams must be given problems to solve, not solutions to build. Often, these "solutions" are expressed as requirements or feature specifications. But if requirements are the wrong way to go, what's the right way? The right way is to understand and express the problem that stakeholders or clients are trying to solve. This is what *business problem statements* do. Business problem statements reframe the work in a way that explicitly demands that product discovery work take place.

While there is some flexibility in what a business problem statement can look like, at the very least it should:

- Provide a specific challenge for the team to solve rather than a set of features to implement.
- Anchor the team in a customer-centric perspective so that customer success is a baked-in part of the end goal.
- Focus the team's effort by specifying guidelines and constraints that make it clear to the team what is in scope and what is out of scope.
- Provide clear measures of success expressed as key performance indicators of the business (desired impacts) or specific outcomes the company wants to see in its target audience.
- Not define a solution (this is surprisingly harder than it sounds).

Foundationally, business problem statements contain three parts:

1. **The current goals of the product or the system the team is working on.** In other words, why was it created in the first place? What problem was it originally designed to solve? What value was it intended to deliver?
2. **What's changed in the world and how that has negatively affected the product?** In other words, where are the goals we set for this product not being met now?
3. **An explicit request to improve the product** that stays away from specifying a solution and that quantifies "improvement" in terms of outcomes.

When you are creating business problem statements, remember that your initial efforts are likely to be filled with assumptions. You'll discover that this is going to be true for every part of the Lean UX Canvas. This is OK; in fact, it's inevitable. Just keep in mind that, as you start to work on the problem—that is, as you start to do the discovery work—you may uncover evidence that you're working on the wrong problem or targeting the wrong audience or measuring success in the wrong way. That's fine. That's why you do discovery! Just make sure you bring this learning back to the team and to stakeholders as soon as you can so that you ensure you're not wasting time and effort on an invalid problem statement.

Facilitating the Exercise

To create a business problem statement, you can certainly sit down informally with stakeholders and product owners to draft one together. That said, we like to do this as part of a workshop setting with the whole team. If you're doing that, we recommend using the following process.

Provide context and background for the team. This often falls on the product manager and is critical to framing the work correctly. Questions that the product manager should answer for the team prior to writing a business problem statement include:

- What have we observed and measured that leads us to believe there's an issue?
- Who are we targeting with this work?
- How does this piece of work fit into the broader program of work the company is undertaking?
- What is the impact of fixing (and not fixing) this problem on company health?

If you have a large group, divide into pairs or trios and write the first draft of the business problem statement in small groups. Small groups can do this together. Spend no more than 30 minutes on this first draft.

Here is the template we use for writing good business problem statements for *existing products*:

> [Our service/product] was designed to achieve [these business/customer goals and deliver this value]. We have observed [in these ways] that the product/service isn't meeting these goals, which is causing [this adverse effect/problem] to our business.
>
> How might we improve service/product so that our customers are more successful as determined by [these measurable changes in their behavior]?

If you're working on *brand new initiatives*, the template looks like this:

> The current state of [the domain we are working in] has focused mainly on [these customer segments, these pain points, these workflows, etc.].
>
> What existing products/services fail to address is [this gap or change in the marketplace].
>
> Our product/service will address this gap by [this product strategy or approach].
>
> Our initial focus will be [this audience segment].
>
> We'll know we are successful when we see [these measurable behaviors in our target audience].

Once the pairs or trios complete their first draft, come back together as a team and read your drafts to each other. Provide critique and feedback, and ask clarifying questions about each draft. Remember that critique isn't a direct attack on the work but rather a clarifying probe to better understand what the authors meant.

Once everyone has shared their draft, combine into larger groups of four to five team members and consolidate into one statement draft. After 30 minutes of subgroup consolidation, share back the reworked drafts with the broader team. Finally, spend 30 more minutes bringing the drafts together into one pan-team business problem statement. Remember that this is an assumptions declaration exercise. Inevitably, some of these assumptions will be wrong, so the goal of Box 1 isn't writing the perfect problem statement. The goal is to begin to build alignment within the team about where you're headed on this initiative and how you'll know you've achieved the goal.

NOTE

Remember that business problem statements are ultimately about the project charter, so if stakeholders haven't been involved, you'll need to bring them in at this point to get their commitment.

Add your completed problem statement draft to your canvas.

Some Examples of Problem Statements

Here is an example of what a good business problem statement looks like:

> When we launched our small and medium-sized (SMB) digital lending solutions, the market consisted of antiquated products sold by legacy banking institutions. In that world, our digital-first lending solutions stood apart and attracted SMB customers searching for new ways to work with their bank. With traditional banks functioning increasingly as "fintech" companies, our market has become crowded and highly competitive. This is causing our customer acquisition costs to go up, market share to stagnate, and customer support costs to rise.
>
> How might we redesign our SMB product line so that our customers believe we are purposefully designed to support their modern businesses, in turn driving our acquisition costs down and market share up?

This example is relatively high-level. It is designed to address a problem at the business unit level. It is important that the team that works on this problem has the jurisdiction and influence to affect work at this level. Writing business problem statements that teams cannot actually solve because they lack the required level of influence is setting that team up to fail.

Here is an example of a more tactical business problem statement that can be assigned to a feature-level team:

> The password retrieval functionality was implemented to help customers quickly get back into the product in the event of a lost or expired password. In addition, this added self-service would reduce the numbers of calls to the customer service center, reducing our overall annual support calls since password reset calls make up at least 35% of inbound calls.
>
> We've noticed through analytics reports and consistent usability study feedback that our customers struggle to find the password retrieval function and, even when they do, fail to complete the reset process on their own at least 42% of the time due to its complexity. This is causing an increase in call center support costs by 12% while exacerbating customer dissatisfaction with our product, potentially leading to a 0.7% increase in churn rate.
>
> How might we redesign the password retrieval experience so that our users are more successful as determined by 90% process completion rates and 50% reduction in calls to customer support about password reset?

What to Watch Out For

Don't specify the solution. the exercise being called a business *problem* statement, we often see teams inserting solutions into the statement. This often shows up in the "how might we" part of the statement with phrases such as "How might we implement a mobile app that solves for this..." Solutions should not be in this exercise at all. We reserve that conversation for Box 5.

Get the level right. We mentioned "leveling" the problem statement correctly earlier, but it's worth repeating that whether you are writing your own problem statements together as a team or someone is writing them for you, your team should only sign up for a problem statement they are capable of solving. If the problem is framed at too high a level, the team will not be able to solve the problem on its own. This will lead to frustration—not only with and within the team but with the overall Lean UX process itself.

Be specific. Another common antipattern is a lack of specificity in the statement. On occasion, teams will leave explicit metrics or evidence out of the problem statement. Specifics are important for framing the importance of the problem as well as setting clear, business-level success criteria for the team. When in doubt, always push for specificity in the statement.

Finally, specificity is important not just to the metrics but for the product area being addressed. Teams will use phrases like "intuitive UI" or "great user experience" to describe work that was done or that is expected to be done. In all cases, phrases like these describe features (albeit in the abstract) that in general should be left out of problem statements.

Here are two examples of phrases like these in business problem statements and how to correct them:

> When we set out to improve our shopping experience, we implemented an intuitive UI for increasing average order value.

In this example, it's not clear what was implemented, so therefore the team doesn't really know what portions of the UI to potentially target for improvement.

In this next example, the ambiguous phrase ends up in the "how might we" portion that seems benign enough but already focuses the team on a specific solution before any discovery work has been done:

> How might we create a more intuitive UI so that customers add more items to their shopping cart during every visit?

You can see here that the framing of the work tells the team to only go after UI enhancements rather than looking for the root cause of dwindling average order values.

--- **NOTE** ---

And for what it's worth, everyone sets out to ship intuitive UIs. No one ever says, "We're going to ship a crappy user interface for the ecommerce platform."

CHAPTER 6

Box 2: Business Outcomes

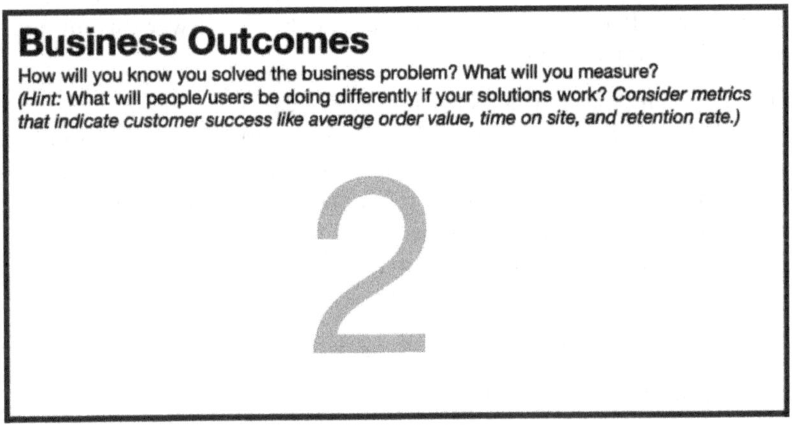

Business Outcomes

How will you know you solved the business problem? What will you measure?
(Hint: What will people/users be doing differently if your solutions work? *Consider metrics that indicate customer success like average order value, time on site, and retention rate.)*

2

Figure 6-1. *Box 2 of the Lean UX Canvas: Business Outcomes*

We covered the concept of outcomes in Chapter 3. Box 2 is where they make their first appearance on the Lean UX Canvas. Once you've got a business problem statement, you want to dig deeper into the core behavior changes you're seeking as part of the initiative. Typically, the success criteria in a problem statement are high-level. Success criteria there tend to be key performance indicators or impact metrics—the things that are found on executive dashboards. These could be metrics like revenue, profit, cost of goods sold, and customer satisfaction. These are helpful at measuring the health of the business, but feature-level teams need to work at a lower level.

In this exercise we work together to uncover the leading indicators of those impact metrics. The question we're trying to answer is *what will people be doing differently if our solutions work?* If we choose the right combination of code, copy, and design, what do we expect to happen? The answers to these questions are what we're looking for in this assumption declaration exercise.

Every option in this brainstorm should start with a verb, and each answer should be something valuable that customers do in the system already, something that's not valuable that we'd like them to do less of, or something new that we think will be valuable and that we'd like them to start doing. In essence, we're thinking through and highlighting user journeys.

Using the User Journey

The goal of this exercise is to find the valuable customer behaviors that we want to focus on. In order to do that, it's helpful to start with a model of customer behavior—what are people doing today? What are they trying to do that's difficult? What are they doing today that's not productive for them or for us? What new, valuable behaviors can we unlock? To answer this question, we can use the idea of user journeys.

User journey mapping can be very simple. We can use a template, like Pirate Metrics or Metrics Mountain (both described below). Or we can use tools that we borrow from Service Design to create a user journey map. Regardless of the framework we choose, the idea is to gather the team and stakeholders around the map and generate a shared understanding of the journey of how people move through our system and which parts of that journey should be the focus of our work.

Depending on your circumstances, here are some models to get you started.

User Journey Type: Pirate Metrics

One way of coming up with your outcome metrics is using Pirate Metrics. Conceived at startup incubator 500 Startups, the Pirate Metrics funnel has become a standard way to think about the user journey through our products. We can use it here to help us determine which portions of that journey are relevant to the problem we're addressing.

Pirate Metrics are made up of five types of customer behaviors:

Acquisition
> These are the activities that get customers to the product in the first place. Viable options here include number of downloads, visits to the registration page, number of sign-ups, etc.

Activation

Once a customer has been acquired, we can start to measure whether or not they are actually using the product. Activation metrics include things like number of accounts created, number of people followed, percentage of new sign-ups that made a purchase, etc. These metrics should reflect the core functionality of the product.

Retention

If we can get customers to try the product, the next challenge is to get them to continue using it on a regular basis. "Regular basis" in this case will be contextual to your product. (For a product like Netflix, you would measure daily viewing habits, but if you make a smart "learning" thermostat, you'd likely measure how few interactions the user had with the device.) If we're retaining customers, generally speaking, they're coming back frequently to use the product, they're doing more in the product, and they're spending time too.

Revenue

If we got them to the product, convinced them to try it, and now they're using it regularly, are they paying us? That's the next level of commitment we look for in our customers. Our goal is to see where and how we're converting customers into paid users and how those patterns evolve over time. Metrics to consider here include percentage of paid versus free users, average lifetime value of each customer, etc.

Referral

The final step in the Pirate Metrics funnel is assessing whether our customers are referring others to the product. If they truly love it, feel like they're getting value from it, and can't live without it, they'll tell their friends or the internet through reviews. This is the best kind of marketing you can get. Metrics to track here include percentage of new users who came through referral, percentage of current users who refer others, and cost of acquisition per new user.

At this point you've probably noticed that the acronym for this method spells AARRR, which is, apparently, how pirates talk, hence the name Pirate Metrics. We can confidently say that neither of us has ever met a pirate, and therefore we cannot confirm that this is indeed pirate-speak.

User Journey Type: Metrics Mountain

One of the things that's bothered us for a while about Pirate Metrics is its visualization as a funnel. In the real world, everything you put into a funnel comes out of that funnel. It takes a bit longer, but the idea that some of the liquid (for example) that you pour at the top of the funnel won't make it out the bottom is ridiculous. Of course it will. There's a hole at the other end! There had to be a better metaphor.

Instead of a funnel, we present Metrics Mountain (Figure 6-2).

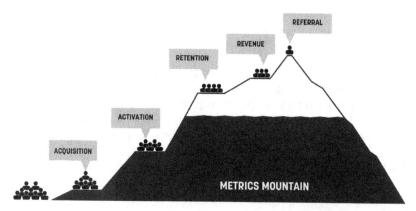

Figure 6-2. *Metrics Mountain. Concept by Jeff Patton and Jeff Gothelf.*

The idea of a mountain to visualize the customer life cycle makes perfect sense because our goal is to get as many of our customers to the top of the mountain. Realistically, though, we're going to lose people along the way. They'll get tired. They'll get bored. They'll get distracted. They'll defect to a competitor. Not every one of them will make it through (i.e., where the funnel metaphor breaks).

As your customers make their way up Metrics Mountain, they are asked to do more and more with your product or service (the climb gets harder). Your goal is to make that as easy a process as possible and to motivate them to keep going. Some of them will do that—especially if you have a compelling value proposition, user experience, and business model. But increasingly, as your customers make their way up the mountain, they will drop off. Our goal should be to build the kinds of experiences that get the highest percentage of people to the top of the mountain.

Facilitating Your Business Outcomes Conversation with Metrics Mountain

You can use the mountain metaphor to facilitate the conversation with your team and stakeholders about the behaviors you believe your users should be progressing through as they use your product. Here's how to do that:

1. Start at the base and identify the first thing a user has to do to begin using your product. How do you acquire them? How do they find the new feature you're working on?

2. Define a "plateau" on the mountain for each subsequent step of your customer journey and determine the user behavior it takes to get there.

3. What percentage of users moving their way up the mountain would your team consider successful for each step? Add those numbers to the mountain diagram.

   - For example, of the 100% of your daily visitors, you would like to see at least 75% discover the new feature you're building, and 50% of those folks give it a try. From there, you'd like to see at least 25% of those who tried to continue using the feature on a weekly basis, with 10% of them ultimately paying you for this new capability.

4. If you're not sure about your exact customer journey, start with Pirate Metrics as the five "ledges" of the mountain. This is a good way to kick off this exercise.

User Journey Type: Service Journeys and User Story Maps

Sometimes, visualizing the user journey as a funnel or a mountain doesn't make sense. You know your product well, and these models may not apply to you. Don't force it. Instead, you can build a Service Journey Map or User Story Map that more closely maps the way a user moves through your product or service. The form isn't really important here: use the method that makes sense for you and your product. The goal is to be able to visualize the flow through the product in a way that you can all see and understand, then use that model to zoom in on the most important parts of the journey, identify the specific behaviors crucial to the success of your initiative, and determine the outcome metrics that would indicate success for that journey.

Outcome-to-Impact Mapping

Outcome-to-impact mapping is another technique to visualize the connection between the impact metrics in your business problem statement and the tactical outcomes you hope to see in your customers. It works well with your feature-level team and is also a powerful exercise to do together with your stakeholders.

This exercise also visualizes the concept of leading and lagging indicators. You'll find that impact metrics are more often lagging indicators—backward-looking measures of what's already taken place. As this exercise progresses, you'll find many of the lower-level metrics, the outcomes, to be leading indicators. These behaviors are often the things that need to take place before we can achieve the impact metric. For example, a customer must first download our app before they can spend money on our service. The former is a leading indicator of the latter. What teams often find is there are many leading indicators for one or two impact metrics. This exercise helps shed light on that fact and forces a (hopefully) productive conversation about prioritization.

Here's how it works:

1. Gather the team and the product leads into a meeting room.

2. On a whiteboard, ask the highest paid person in the room to write down the current strategic goal for the year at the top on a series of Post-it notes.

3. Below that, ask that same person (or another executive) to list out the measures of success for that strategy (hint: these should be impact metrics and are often lagging indicators).

4. Below each impact metric, start to draw lines protruding away from each one (like you're building an org chart).

5. Ask the room to fill out the line below the impact metrics with customer behaviors that drive those metrics (leading indicators). Use Post-its and have everyone work individually on an initial brainstorm.

6. Now have the team do another row below the last one showing the customer behaviors that drive the initial set of outcomes.

At this point, your whiteboard should start to look like the map shown in Figure 6-3:

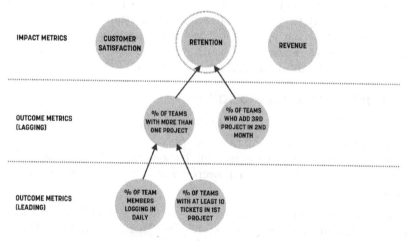

Figure 6-3. *Outcome-to-impact mapping*

Once everyone's contributed, you should have dozens of Post-its on the board indicating a variety of customer behaviors (outcomes) that will help your company hit its strategic goal and impact targets. Also at this point, your team may be overwhelmed. Most times we've run this exercise, it never occurs to the team that there are so many ways to potentially drive positive change.

Now, the tough part. Through a round of dot voting (or other facilitated selection exercise), ask the team to pick the 10 outcomes they think they should focus on first.

What you've done here is create a direct connection between outcomes (customer behaviors) and impact metrics (the thing executives care about) and forced them to choose where you should focus for the next cycle. The last step is to create a baseline for each of these outcomes (i.e., where they are today) and a goal (i.e., where we'd like them to be at the end of the cycle) and assign them to the team as goals for their next cycle.

Now, each time a team reports progress on their specific outcome, their stakeholder will have a clear sense of *why* the team is working on that and *how* it affects the impact metrics they care most about.

What to Watch Out For

Not every number or percentage is an outcome metric. Jeff was working with a huge German retail conglomerate on this specific exercise. Their impact-level goal was to increase same store sales year over year. As we worked through the outcome-to-impact mapping exercise, a few team members added items to the outcome rows that read "percentage of products on the shelf that are our brand." Now, technically, this is a metric, but it is not a measure of customer behavior. It is a product strategy decision that you hope will drive some customer behavior. A similar issue came up once with another client building an automation tool. A person on the team listed "percentage of manual tasks now automated by the system." Again, this is not a measure of customer behavior. It's a facet of the system being built, a product decision. The ultimate goal was to reduce the amount of time staff spent on repetitive tasks—which *is* a good outcome metric.

The other thing we've seen often is that these charts get messy. It's easy to make them look neat in a book or PowerPoint slide. In reality, our businesses aren't this linear, and these charts can get a bit unwieldy (Figure 6-4). Teams will often find that one outcome drives multiple impact metrics (this is perfectly reasonable) and has to be duplicated across the chart. Build the chart that works for your business and your team. Just don't compromise the content of the exercise.

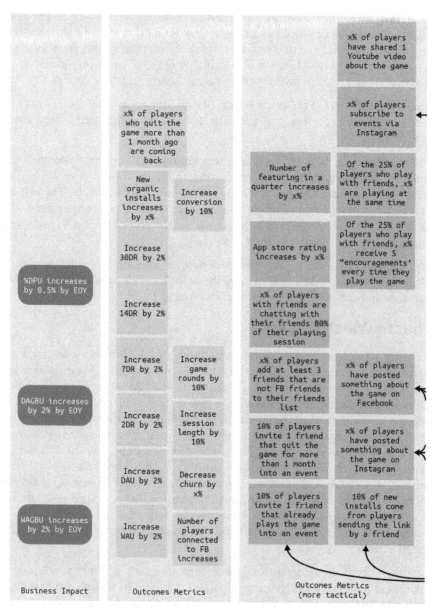

Figure 6-4. *Real world example of an outcome to impact map, courtesy of Delphine Sassi and the team at King*

CHAPTER 7

Box 3: Users

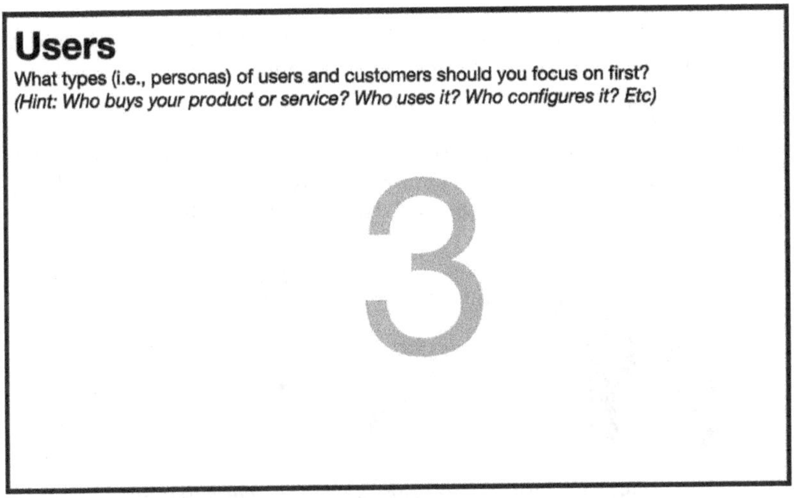

Users

What types (i.e., personas) of users and customers should you focus on first?
(Hint: Who buys your product or service? Who uses it? Who configures it? Etc)

3

Figure 7-1. Box 3 of the Lean UX Canvas: Users

Designers have long been advocates for the end user. Lean UX doesn't change that. As we make assumptions about our business and the outcomes we'd like to achieve, we still need to keep the user front and center in our thinking. Box 3 of the canvas begins a deeper conversation into our target audience.

Most of us learned to think about a persona as a tool to represent what we learned in our research. And it was often the case that we created personas as the output of lengthy, expensive research studies. There are a few problems with personas that are created this way.

First, we tend to regard them as untouchable because of all of the work that went into creating them. In addition, it's often the case that these personas were created by a research team or third-party vendor. This creates a risky knowledge gap between the people who conducted the research and those who are using the personas.

In Lean UX, we change the order of operations in the persona process. We also change persona creation from a one-time activity to an ongoing process—one that takes place whenever we learn something new about our users.

When creating personas in this approach, we start with assumptions and then do research to validate our assumption. Instead of spending months in the field interviewing people, we spend a few hours creating proto-personas. Proto-personas are our best guess as to who is using (or will use) our product and why. We sketch them on paper with the entire team contributing—we want to capture everyone's assumptions. Then, as we conduct ongoing research, we quickly find out how accurate our initial guesses are, and we adjust our personas in response.

Besides putting the customer front and center for a diverse product development team, proto-personas serve two more key purposes.

Shared understanding

Imagine your team sitting around a table and someone says the word "dog." What image comes to your mind? Is it the same image that comes to your colleagues' minds (Figure 7-2)? How do you know?

Figure 7-2. *Dogs. We are indebted to our learned colleague Adrian Howard for this concept.*

The same thing happens when someone says, "the user." The proto-persona approach ensures that everyone has the same image in their head when "the user" is invoked.

Remembering we are not the user

It is often easy to assume our users are like us—especially if we consume the products we make. The reality is that we have a level of understanding and tolerance for the technology that our customers rarely share. Going through a proto-persona exercise puts the focus on external users, pushing the team further away from their personal preferences for the product.

Using Proto-Personas

A team we were working with in New York was building an app that improved the Community Supported Agriculture (CSA) experience for New York City residents. CSA is a program that allows city residents to pool their money and purchase an entire season's worth of produce from a local farmer. The farmer then delivers crops weekly to the members of the CSA. Many subscribers to the CSA are people in their late 20s and early 30s who need to juggle a busy work life, an active social life, and a desire to participate in the CSA.

The team assumed that most CSA consumers were women who liked to cook. They spent about an hour creating a persona named Susan. But when they went out into the field to do research with young professionals in their 20s, they quickly learned that the overwhelming majority of cooks, and hence potential users of their app, were young men. They returned to the office and revised their persona to create Anthony.

Anthony proved to be a far more accurate target user. The team had not wasted any more time refining ideas for the wrong audience. They were now focused on an audience that, while still not perfect, was far more correct than their initial assumptions.

The Proto-Persona Template

We like to sketch proto-personas on paper using three hand-drawn sections (Figure 7-3). The upper-left quadrant holds a rough sketch of the persona along with a name and role. The upper-right box holds basic demographic, psychographic, and behavioral information. One antipattern for personas that we see is an overemphasis on demographics. For product design, we care less about demographics and more about needs, goals, and behaviors. So when you're thinking about demographics, try to focus on information that predicts a specific type of behavior—behavior relevant to our product or service. For example, there might be cases for which the persona's age is totally irrelevant, whereas their access to a specific device, like an iPhone, will completely change the way they interact with your product. We only want to write down the "differences that make a difference."

· MARRIED
· 2 KIDS
· FOCUSED ON KID'S
  KID'S HEALTH & SCHOOL
· DISPOSABLE INCOME

TIM
39 YRS
OLD
"DAD"

NEEDS/OBSTACLES

- NEEDS TO UNDERSTAND WHAT KIDS
  DO IN SCHOOL

- NEEDS A CLEAR, ONGOING ASSESSMENT
  OF KID

· OBSTACLE: ACCESS TO TEACHERS

· OBSTACLE: OUTDATED SCHOOL TECH TOOLS

· WANTS TO HELP CHILD LEARN

Figure 7-3. A completed proto-persona template

The bottom half of the proto-persona is where we put the most important details. Here we capture the goals, needs, desired outcomes, and obstacles that keep them from achieving these needs. Remember that users rarely need "features." What they need is to attain some kind of goal. (It's not always a concrete goal: sometimes it's an emotional goal, an unarticulated desire, etc.) It is our job to decide how best to get them to their goals.

Facilitating the Exercise

Once again, we like to start the persona creation process with a brainstorm:

1. Team members start by offering up their opinions on who the project should be targeting and how that would affect their use of the product.

2. The team creates a list of persona types.

For example, this list could contain target segments like "college students," "streaming enthusiasts," "front-line medical workers," etc.

3. Narrow down the ideas to an initial set of three to four personas the team believes are most likely to be their target audience.

4. Try to differentiate the personas around needs and roles rather than by demographic information.

5. After you've narrowed down the list of potential users, have the team complete a proto-persona template for each one.

   You can break into small groups and have each group focus on one persona, then bring these back to the group to review.

6. Revise each persona based on feedback.

Once you have a set of personas that you agree on, share with your colleagues beyond the team for their input.

Early Validation

At this point in the process, you can begin to validate some of your early assumptions. In fact, before you get too much further declaring assumptions, this is a good spot to start testing some of those assumptions. Use your personas as recruiting targets to begin your research.

Immediately, there are three things you can determine based on your proto-personas:

Does the customer exist?
   By recruiting for the personas you created, you can quickly determine how realistic your team's assumptions are. If you can't find the people you sketched, they probably don't exist. Learn from that and edit your personas.

Do they have the needs and obstacles you think they do?
   In other words, are we solving real problems? You can gauge this simply by observing and speaking with the individuals you recruit. If these conversations and observations don't confirm the problem, then you're building solutions for problems that don't exist—and that rarely ends well.

Would they value a solution to this problem?
   Just because a customer is real and has the pain points you're solving for, it doesn't actually mean they'll value a new way to solve that problem. In other words, just because they eat bananas on their cereal every day and they don't like slicing bananas, it doesn't mean that they'll buy your banana slicer (Figure 7-4). It's important to understand how your customers are currently solving these needs and how likely your idea is to displace

the incumbent solution. If you're trying to displace long-held tools like email or spreadsheets, you might be in for a tough fight. It's good to get that information sooner rather than later.

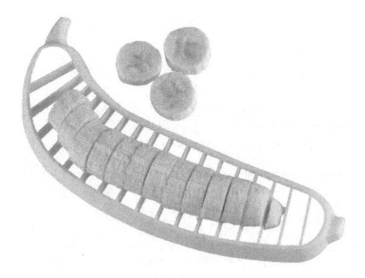

Figure 7-4. *The banana slicer. Who buys these?*

We once worked with a startup that serviced the needs of angel investors by creating an online repository for all things related to their investments. It was a robust product that promised to streamline and simplify the lives of these users. Upon joining the project, we worked with the team to build proto-personas, and we set out to find the target audience. Turns out, this wasn't a challenge at all. In the United States, at least, there are many folks who qualify as angel investors (i.e., they have an extra $50–100K sitting around to invest). The persona exists!

Next, we started speaking with these people to understand if we were solving a real problem for them. Turns out that, yes indeed, tracking pitch decks, term sheets, cap tables, and follow-on round information was tedious for this audience. The problem exists! This was getting exciting.

Finally, the team began to pick up on a trend when the conversation turned to digital solutions to this problem. The overwhelming majority of our target audience—something close to 95%—invested once or twice a year, maximum. For one or two investments per year, email and Microsoft Excel worked just fine. Our audience was intimately familiar with these tools, and no amount of robustness, complexity, or even ease of use of our online investment management tool was going to move our audience off email and Excel in favor of our product. The tool we were building was for the 5% of investors for whom this was a profession—a population far too small to justify the effort being put into the product being built. That was a tough conversation to have back at the office, as you can imagine. Just because the persona exists and you're solving a real problem for them doesn't always mean they'll value the solution you're building. Better to find that out now, at Box 3 in the Lean UX Canvas, than once you've started shipping code to production.

What to Watch Out For

Many teams we've worked with and heard from over the years run this proto-persona exercise; however, far fewer of them actually go back and adjust their thinking after the initial creation exercise. It is important that you consider proto-personas to be living documents. Each time you conduct customer conversations or usability studies, ask yourself how many of the team's current beliefs about their target audience are still true. As new information is revealed, bring it up for discussion and adjust the personas so that future research efforts can be more targeted and more successful.

CHAPTER 8

Box 4: User Outcomes and Benefits

User Outcomes & Benefits
Why would your users seek out your product or service? What benefit would they gain from using it? What behavior change can we observe that tells us they've achieved their goal? *(Hint: Save money, get a promotion, spend more time with family)*

4

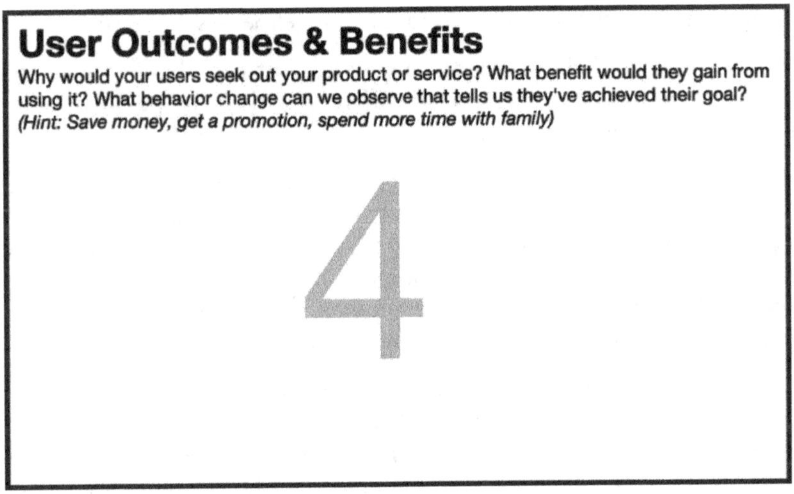

Figure 8-1. *Box 4 of the Lean UX Canvas: User Outcomes and Benefits*

Despite the proliferation of Agile techniques like user stories, the user and their goals often become lost in the lengthy debates over features, designs, and technical implementations. Empathy is at the heart of great products and services. Designers often have been responsible for advocating for the user from an empathetic point of view. As we now know, this is not uniquely a designer's responsibility. To achieve broader shared understanding of users and a deeper sense of empathy for what they are trying to achieve, we ask our teams to declare their assumptions about what users are trying to do, in the form of user outcomes and benefits.

Before starting Box 4, you may be asking yourself, what's the difference between business outcomes, customer outcomes, and user outcomes? Good question. Let's take a look at an example in which you work for a company that makes corporate expense tracking software.

The business outcome the company is trying to achieve is to acquire more customers, retain the ones they already have, and increase monthly software subscription revenue.

The *customers* of this company—other companies who buy the expense tracking software for their employees—are trying to improve the efficiency of their accounting teams, reduce payment of expenses that are not reimbursable, and drive down overall operational costs.

The *users* of the software are the employees at these customer companies. Their desired goal is to get their expenses reimbursed as quickly as possible and reduce the time it takes them to input those expenses correctly.

All of these are still behavior-based outcomes, but each has its own point of view. In other words, they refer to the different goals being pursued by the different groups of people.

In addition to behavior change, there are emotional goals at both the customer and user levels. The *buyers* of this software want to feel like they are helping the company be more successful and profitable. They want to look good to their bosses and want to be able to point to their specific contributions to the success of the company. This would motivate them to seek out a brand of expense tracking software that allows them to do this easily.

The *users* of the software want to get reimbursed quickly and feel confident their expenses will be fully reimbursed without a myriad of red tape and corporate hassle. This would motivate these users to be more diligent and deliberate in the use of this software rather than having it be yet another corporate IT tool that goes unused or worked around.

It's worth noting that all of these outcomes are important and should be called out specifically as business, customer, or user outcomes. However, not all of these are quantifiable. Meeting users' emotional goals is hard—particularly if the team tends to focus on metrics, because you measure these emotional factors in different ways. That said, just because it's hard, doesn't mean you shouldn't pay attention to this type of goal. These emotional goals are critical: they're the ones that help teams understand what kind of experience they're trying to deliver and ultimately, if you get it right, will lead to better performance on the quantifiable metrics.

Facilitating the Exercise

Once your proto-personas have been created, you can use the material in the bottom portion of the proto-persona as the basis for this discussion. Working individually, in small groups, or as a whole team, work your way through each proto-persona. Use the following questions as your prompts:

What is the user trying to accomplish?
Example answer: I want to buy a new phone.

How does the user want to feel during and after this process?
Example answer: I want to feel like I got the phone that I need at a good price and that I'm keeping up with my peers (i.e., I want to feel cool).

How does our product or service get the user closer to a life goal or dream?
Example answer: I want to feel tech-savvy and respected for it.

Why would your user seek out your product?
Example answer: I want to fit in with my friends at school.

What behavior change can we observe that tells they've achieved their goal?
Example answer: They bring their new phone to school every day.

Note that not every user outcome exists at all levels. But thinking about outcomes in these terms can help you to find important dimensions of your solution to work on, from the functional, task-oriented outcomes to the more emotional experience-oriented outcomes.

This section of the canvas is where the team digs into the emotional side of the conversation. We're not talking about features, pixels, or code here. We want to understand what would drive our personas to look for our product and, when they find it, what they might do. When the time comes to begin testing, marketing, or advertising the product, the work we do in this section becomes a gold mine for content, calls-to-action, and helpful instructional text.

What to Watch Out For

Sometimes teams get so feature-focused that this exercise becomes a bit of a recursive exercise. We've seen teams write down features in this section because they assume that's what motivates their customers. Writing down a user benefit as "calendar integration" misses the point of this exercise. The goal here is to understand the user's latent needs. "Never be late to another meeting" is far more important and compelling for the user than the specifics of the feature that will help them do that. Apple is always very good at differentiating the iPhone this way against Samsung and other competitors. While the competition is touting features like "12-megapixel camera," Apple advertises, "Show grandma the baby from across the country."

CHAPTER 9

Box 5: Solutions

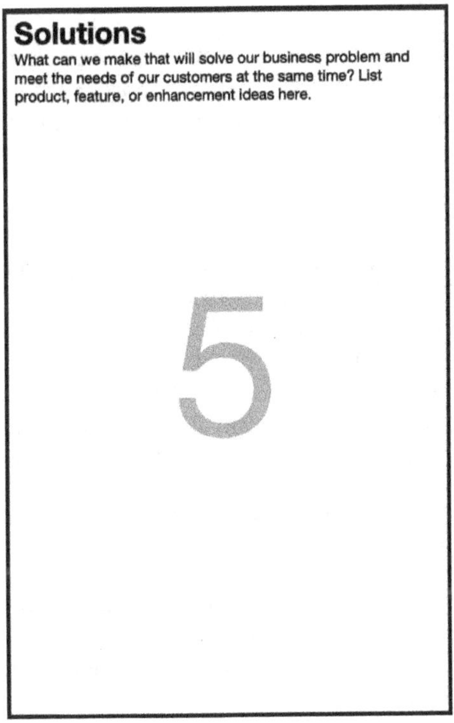
Solutions
What can we make that will solve our business problem and meet the needs of our customers at the same time? List product, feature, or enhancement ideas here.
5

Figure 9-1. *Box 5 of the Lean UX Canvas: Solutions*

Finally we've arrived at the point in the Lean UX process when we get to talk about solutions. This is by design. While we certainly could have started our work discussing the solutions or features we'd like to build (and, most often, that's where projects start: with required solutions!), our work is better when we step back and put some constraints in place. In our case, we've set constraints with our business problem statement, business outcomes, the persona work we've done, and our discussion of user outcomes and benefits. Without those constraints, solutions will either solve the wrong problem for the wrong people or end up scattered and unfocused. Each set of assumptions we've declared so far has constrained the space in which we can create solutions, and creativity thrives in constraints.

We're still not getting into detailed design work here. That comes once we complete the canvas. However, we do start getting specific on what we believe will get us and our customers from their current condition to the target condition.

Facilitating the Exercise

As with most of these assumptions declaration exercises, there are multiple ways to facilitate them. We've listed several approaches below to help you get started, but feel free to add your favorite design brainstorming techniques to help you and your team complete Box 5.

Affinity Mapping

Affinity mapping is the simplest and easiest way to get the team working together in Box 5. Have each person work individually to brainstorm solution ideas that would solve the business problem and achieve the desired business and user outcomes for your target persona. Each person should generate as many ideas as they can come up with, putting one idea per Post-it note. As with any brainstorming activity, it's only as good as the framing question used to solicit responses. In this case, the question to pose to your team is:

> What solutions can we design and build that will serve our personas and create their desired outcomes?

Each person can write words or create small sketches on the Post-it notes for five minutes. The team then shares their ideas with each other, sorting similar ideas into groups before dot voting which approaches they believe stand the greatest chance for success.

While affinity mapping will get you through the process the fastest, taking your time here can yield additional benefits beyond just identifying high-level solution ideas.

Collaborative Design: A More Structured Approach

A more deliberate way to develop solutions ideas is a collaborative design method that we call Design Studio. (We write more about collaborative design methods, including Design Sprints, in Chapter 14.) When you need to gather everyone for a formal working session, Design Studio is a popular way to do this.

This method, born in the architecture world where it was called Design Charrette, is a way to bring a cross-functional team together to visualize potential solutions to a design problem. It breaks down organizational silos and creates a forum for your fellow teammates' points of view.

By putting designers, developers, subject-matter experts, product managers, business analysts, and other competencies together in the same space, focused on the same challenge, you create an outcome far greater than working in silos allows. It has another benefit. It begins to build the trust your team will need to move from these formal sessions to more frequent and informal collaborations.

Running a Design Studio

The technique described in the sections that follow is very specific; however, you should feel comfortable to run less or more formal Design Studios as your situation and timing warrants. The specifics of the ritual are not the point as much as the activity of solving problems with your colleagues and clients. Regardless of which approach you choose, remember that the goal is to come up with solution ideas that solve your business problem.

Setting

To run a Design Studio session, you'll want to find a dedicated block of time within which you can bring the team together. You should plan on at least a three-hour block. You'll want a room with tables that folks can gather around. The room should have good wall space, so you can post the work in progress to the walls as you go.

If you're working in a remote session, use a good team whiteboard tool like Mural or Miro. Remember to spend some time making sure that everyone is comfortable with the tool you choose—you may have to spend some time at the start of the meeting to bring everyone up to speed on the tools.

The Team

This process works best for a team of five to eight people. If you have more people, you can create more teams and have the teams compare output at the end of the process. (Larger groups take a long time to get through the critique and feedback steps, so it's important to split groups larger than about eight people into smaller teams, which can each go through the following process in parallel, converging at the end.)

With remote sessions, this is where a videoconferencing "breakout room" feature comes into play. Since we don't have physical space to divide up, video breakout rooms give each team the privacy and focus it needs to do its own work.

Process

Design Studio works within the following flow:

- Problem definition and constraints
- Individual idea generation (diverge)
- Presentation and critique
- Iterate and refine in pairs (emerge)
- Team idea generation (converge)

Supplies

For in-person session, here are the supplies you'll need:

- Pencils
- Pens
- Felt-tip markers or similar (multiple colors/thickness)
- Highlighters (multiple colors)
- Sketching templates (you can use preprinted one-up and six-up templates, or you can use blank sheets of 11" x 17" [A3] paper divided into six boxes)
- 25" x 30.5" (A1) self-stick easel pads
- Drafting dots (or any kind of small stickers)

With distributed teams, all of these tools become moot in favor of the online collaboration tool you've chosen to use. That said, we've seen some remote facilitators still challenge folks to use paper and pen for initial sketches, photograph those sketches, and share them in the online whiteboard tool after creating it locally.

Problem Definition and Constraints (15 Minutes)

The first step in Design Studio is to ensure that everyone is aware of the assumptions you've declared so far: the business problem you are trying to solve, the outcomes that define success for the effort, the users you are serving, and the benefits they are trying to achieve. In most cases, the team is already aware of this since they've worked on the canvas together up until this point. If you haven't done this work together, plan some extra time for briefing the team and answering their questions.

Individual Idea Generation (10 Minutes)

You'll be working individually in this step. Give each member of the team a six-up template, which is a sheet of paper with six empty boxes on it, as depicted in Figure 9-2. You can make one by folding a blank sheet of 11" x 17" (A3) paper, or make a preprinted template to hand to participants. (If you're using an online tool, don't force people to draw in that tool—that tends to be hard and slow. Instead, ask people to work on paper then share a photo or scan.)

Figure 9-2. A blank "six-up" template

Sometimes, people find they have a hard time facing a blank page. If that's the case, try this optional step. Ask everyone to label each box on their sheets with one of your personas and the specific pain point or problem they will be addressing for that persona. Write the persona's name and pain point at the top of each of the six boxes. You can write the same persona/pain point pair as many times as you have solutions for that problem, or you can write a different persona/pain point combination for each box. Any combination works. Spend five minutes doing this.

Next, with your six-up sheets in front of you, give everyone five minutes to generate six low-fidelity sketches of solutions (see Figure 9-3) for each persona/problem pair on their six-up sheet. These should be visual articulations (UI sketches, workflows, diagrams, etc.) and not written words. Encourage your team by revealing the dirty little secret of interaction design: if you can draw a circle, square, and a triangle, you can draw every interface. We're confident everyone on your team can draw those shapes, and this seemingly silly idea can help level the playing field.

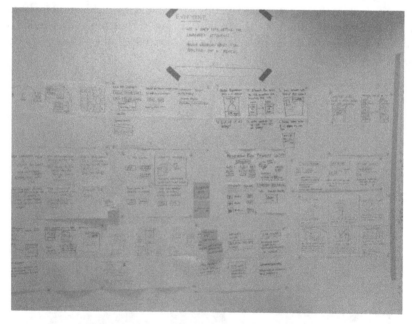

Figure 9-3. *A wall full of completed six-up drawings*

Presentation and Critique (3 Minutes per Person)

When time is up, share and critique what you've done so far. Going around the room, give the participants three minutes to share their sketches and present them to the team (Figure 9-4). Presenters should explicitly state who they were solving a problem for (in other words, what persona) and which pain point they were addressing, and then explain the sketch.

Each member of the team should provide critique and feedback to the presenter. Team members should focus their feedback on clarifying the presenter's intentions.

Help your team understand that giving good feedback is an art. Remind them that, in general, it's better to ask questions than to share opinions. Questions help the team talk about what they're doing and help individuals think through their work. Opinions, on the other hand, can stop the conversation, inhibit collaboration, and put people on the defensive. So when you're providing critique, try to use questions like "How does this feature address the persona's specific problem?" or "I don't understand that part of the drawing. Can you elaborate?" Questions like these are very helpful. Comments such as "I don't like that concept" provide little value and don't give the presenter concrete ideas to use for iterating.

Figure 9-4. *A team presenting and critiquing drawings during a Design Studio*

Pair Up to Iterate and Refine (10 Minutes)

Now ask everyone to pair up for the next round. (If two people in the session had similar ideas, it's a good idea to ask them to work together.) For remote sessions, each pair should work in their own breakout room.

Each pair will be working to revise their design ideas (Figure 9-5). The goal here is to have each pair pick the ideas that have the most merit and develop a more evolved, more integrated version of those ideas. Each pair will have to make some decisions about what to keep, what to change, and what to throw away. Expect that this will be hard and that each pair will disagree about some things. Resist the temptation here to create quick agreement by getting more general or abstract. Instead, ask each pair to make some decisions and get more specific. Have each pair produce a single drawing on an 11" × 17" (A3) six-up sheet. Give each team 10 minutes for this step.

When the time is up, bring everyone together and go through the present-and-critique process again.

Figure 9-5. *A team working together in a Design Studio exercise*

Team Idea Generation (45 Minutes)

Now that all team members have feedback on their individual ideas and people have paired up to develop ideas further, the team must converge on one idea. In this step, the team is trying to select the ideas they feel have the best chance for success. This set of ideas will serve as the basis for the next step in the Lean UX process: creating hypotheses and, eventually, designing and running experiments.

Ask the team to use a large sheet of self-stick easel pad paper or a whiteboard to sketch the components and workflow for their idea. There will be a lot of compromise and wrangling at this stage, and to get to consensus, the team will need to prioritize and pare back features.

Encourage the team to create a "parking lot" for good ideas that don't make the cut. This will make it easier to let go of ideas. Again, it's important to make decisions here: resist the temptation to get consensus by generalizing or deferring decisions.

--- **NOTE** ---

If you have split a large group into multiple teams in the Design Studio, ask each team to present their final idea to the room when they are finished for one final round of critique and feedback and, if desired, convergence.

Using the Output

The work you do in a Design Studio will feed into the creation of hypotheses and ultimately experiment design. This doesn't mean that every single idea will make it into final consideration, but the ideas the team has converged on will all be put to the test starting with Box 6, hypothesis creation.

To keep the output visible, post it on a design wall or another prominent place so that the team can refer back to it. Decide on what (if any) intermediate drawings people want to keep and display these alongside the final drawing, again so that team members can refer back to the ideas. Regardless of what you keep posted on the wall, it's generally a good idea to photograph everything and keep it in an archive folder of some sort. You never know when you'll want to go back to find something. It's also a good idea to put a single person in charge of creating this archive. Creating some accountability will tend to ensure that the team keeps good records.

What to Watch Out For

The toughest part of collaborative design is ensuring even participation. If you keep the exercise simple, most folks will feel like they can participate quite easily. (Everyone can write on a Post-it note.) If you decide to use more involved techniques like Design Studio, you'll need to ensure that facilitation is top notch. (And remember that this will all be more difficult in remote sessions.) If members of your team tune out during this part because they feel like these exercises were too advanced for them, they're likely to put up a much bigger resistance to some of the feature and design choices the team makes downstream. In this instance, as much as anywhere else, design facilitation becomes a core skill set for the designers on your team.

CHAPTER 10

Box 6: Hypotheses

Hypotheses

Combine the assumptions from 2, 3, 4 & 5 into the following hypothesis statement:
"We believe that [business outcome] will be achieved if [user] attains [benefit] with [feature]."
(Hint: Each hypothesis should focus on one feature only.)

6

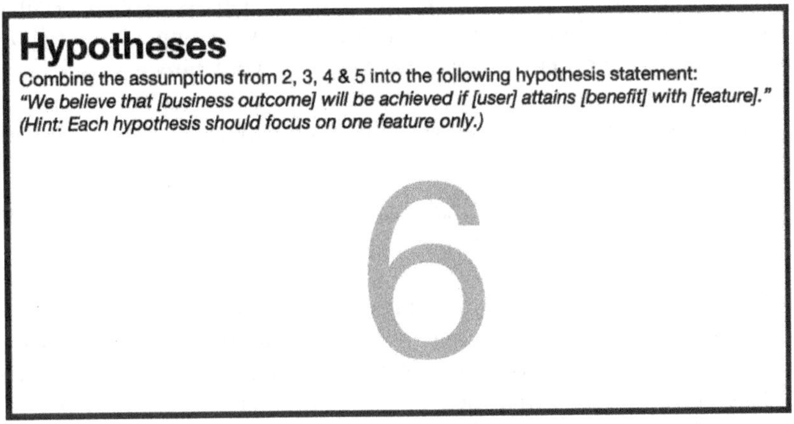

Figure 10-1. *Box 6 of the Lean UX Canvas: Hypotheses*

When the team arrives at Box 6, it has all the raw material it needs to start writing tactical, testable hypotheses. Before we do that, though, let's talk about hypotheses in general.

Hypothesis has become a popular word in product development recently, in no small part because of *The Lean Startup*, in which Eric Ries describes a method of product development inspired by the scientific method. He advocates testing your hypotheses early and often. So what is a hypothesis anyway? According to *The Oxford Dictionary of Difficult Words*, it's "a supposition or proposed explanation made on the basis of limited evidence as a starting point for further investigation."[1]

That's what we're about to create: we're going to take all of our assumptions (assumptions are statements based on "limited evidence"), and we're going to gather them into a unified statement (our "proposed explanation" of our problem and solution) so that we can begin our research and testing process (our "further investigation").

OK, with that out of the way, let's get started writing hypotheses. This is the template we recommend:

> We believe we will achieve [**this business outcome**]
>
> If [**these personas**]
>
> Attain [**this benefit/user outcome**]
>
> With [**this feature or solution**]

The template starts with the words "we believe." This is explicit because we don't know. We're making assumptions. And then we complete the hypothesis template based on the material we've created in every canvas box before this one. We pull business outcomes from Box 2, personas from Box 3, benefits from Box 4, and solutions from Box 5. In some ways, this part of the process is just *fill-in-the-blanks*.

But we need to do a little more than that. Our goal here is to write hypotheses that make sense and that we believe. These hypotheses are, in essence, very short stories designed to build support for pursuing a particular design direction. Writing a good hypothesis that makes sense and that you and your team believe is actually the first way to test the validity of your solution brainstorms. If you can't put together a compelling hypothesis statement for one of the solution ideas in Box 5, then that idea shouldn't graduate to the next part of the process. And, just to be extra clear, a compelling hypothesis is one where the feature has a clear user, the user gets an obvious benefit from the feature, and the subsequent user behavior change helps solve the business problem we articulated in Box 1.

---

1 Archie Hobson (ed.), *The Oxford Dictionary of Difficult Words* (New York: Oxford University Press, 2004), s.v. "hypothesis."

Facilitating the Exercise

We like to create a table like the one in Figure 10-2 and then complete it by using the material we've filled in the earlier parts of the canvas. We physically move our Post-it notes into the appropriate boxes to make rows of related ideas. Each column is directly related to a specific box of the canvas, from Box 2 on the left to Box 5 on the right.

We'll achieve this...	if this persona...	can achieve this...	with this...
BUSINESS OUTCOME	PERSONA	USER OUTCOME	FEATURE

Figure 10-2. *A hypothesis table*

You'll often find during this exercise that there are gaps in your initial brainstorms. Some business outcomes might have no features created for them, whereas some features might not drive any value for the customer or the business. That's part of the point of this exercise: to organize and make sense of your initial round of thinking. After you've identified the gaps in your brainstorms, fill them in with new sticky notes (Figure 10-3) or—even better—leave the less relevant ideas off the chart. This will help make sense of the undoubtedly large number of ideas your team generates.

With distributed teams using a virtual whiteboard tool, this exercise becomes even easier. Copy and paste your notes from other parts of the canvas into Box 6 and move them around as necessary to complete the chart.

Figure 10-3. *Working on the hypothesis chart*

After you've completed the chart—7 to 10 rows are a good initial target—begin extracting feature hypotheses from it. Use the hypothesis template to ensure you're including all the relevant components of the hypothesis statement. Here's that template again:

> We believe we will achieve [**this business outcome**]
>
> If [**these personas**]
>
> Attain [**this benefit/user outcome**]
>
> With [**this feature or solution**]

As you write your hypotheses, consider which persona(s) you're serving with your proposed solutions. It's not unusual to find solutions that serve more than one persona at a time. It's also not unusual to create a hypothesis in which multiple features drive similar outcomes. When you see that happening, refine the hypothesis to focus on just one feature. Hypotheses with multiple features are not easy to test. The important thing to remember in this entire process is to keep your ideas specific enough so that you can create meaningful tests to see if your ideas hold water.

What's the Difference Between Hypotheses and Agile User Stories?

We're often asked to differentiate between hypothesis statements and classic Agile user stories. The difference is subtle but powerful. One of the more popular formats for Agile user stories look like this:

As a <type of user>,

I want <some goal>

so that <some reason>.

You'll notice that the user and user outcome are present in this story. That said, most teams we've worked with replace "some goal" with "this feature." After the user story is written, most teams discard the pieces around "some goal" and begin implementing the feature. The user is quickly forgotten as the team works diligently to drive up their velocity and deliver the feature. The team's acceptance criteria (i.e., their definition of success) is that the system allows the user to complete a task. There is no discussion as to whether the solution is usable or desirable, much less delightful. There's no discussion of whether the feature creates an outcome. The only testing being done is whether the system "works as designed."

Hypotheses have behavior change (business outcomes) as their definition of success. Shipping a working feature is table stakes. It's the beginning of the conversation. Our team's success is not measured by how fast they can get features launched. Instead, we measure success by how well our customers can achieve "some goal" initially and continuously.

This is the key difference between user stories and hypotheses. They refocus the team on what's really important—making the customer successful and thus achieving a business goal—as opposed to measuring team productivity as success.

That said, you still need a way to talk about output and features—the things that the team is building. If your user stories are feature-centric, that's fine. In fact, it's often the case that a given hypothesis results in many user stories. However you decide to track the work is fine. Just make sure that some part of your process connects the work you're doing on the feature level to the higher-level user and business outcomes that you're trying to create.

Prioritizing Hypotheses

Lean UX is an exercise in ruthless prioritization. It's rare to have a project budget focused strictly on learning. In most cases, we need to ship product too. The reason we declare our assumptions at the outset of our work is so that we can identify project risks and prioritize. What's risky and needs testing? What's not risky and thus easy to start?

After we string our assumptions together into hypotheses, we create a backlog of potential work. Next, we need to figure out which ones are the riskiest ones—so that we can work on them first. Understanding that you can't test every assumption, how do you decide which one to test first?

There are lots of ways that you can prioritize, but we've found that it can often be helpful to do this collaboratively and to have a framework to use for this work. That's why we created the Hypothesis Prioritization Canvas shown in Figure 10-4. (Yes, another canvas.) The HPC is a two-by-two matrix with the x-axis measuring risk, and the y-axis measuring perceived value. We use "perceived" value because this is a big assumption. We believe that an idea has high perceived value if its implementation will meaningfully impact the user experience and therefore the business. When it comes to risk, we evaluate each hypothesis on its own merit. Some hypotheses are going to be technically risky. Some will pose risk to the brand. Others will challenge our design capabilities. In this case, we don't normalize for a specific type of risk so we can consider all aspects of risk for each hypothesis.

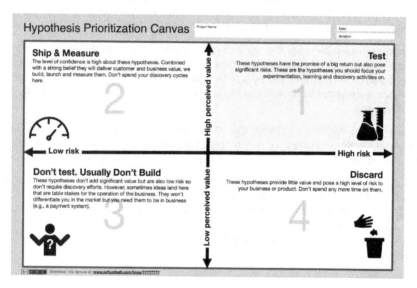

Figure 10-4. *The Hypothesis Prioritization Canvas*

Map your hypotheses on the canvas as a team.

- The hypotheses that land in *quadrant 1* are the hypotheses we are going to test. They graduate to Boxes 7 and 8 in the Lean UX Canvas.

- If a hypothesis lands in *quadrant 2* of the HPC—high value, low risk—we're going to build it. Write the user stories, put them on the backlog, and ship them. But don't forget to measure that feature once it's live. If it doesn't live up to your expectations—aka the business outcomes defined in the hypothesis as success—you need to revisit this idea.

- Any hypothesis that falls below the risk axis into the low perceived value area doesn't get tested. If it lands in *quadrant 4* of the HPC—high risk, low value—we throw it away. No need to build it either.

- Hypotheses that end up in *quadrant 3* of the HPC—low risk, low value—don't get tested and in most cases don't get built. However, there will be some hypotheses that end up here that, while not particularly valuable or risky, still need to get built so you can operate your business. For example, you will have to implement a payment system if you're building an ecommerce service, but that won't differentiate you in the marketplace. In this case, we build the basic use cases knowing that our innovative and delightful features—the riskier features—are going to be tested and validated before implementation.

What to Watch Out For

Hypothesis writing, like most new techniques, gets better with practice. Teams will often write hypotheses that are too big to test early in their Lean UX journey. If you find yourself in this situation, rethink the scope of your hypothesis. How can you make it smaller? How can you size the hypothesis to a point where your team can have total ownership over its scope?

Hypothesis writing, like business problem statement writing, also benefits from specificity. Use specific numbers in your business outcomes. Be clear about the feature you'd like to build. This is another area where phrases like "better user experience" and "intuitive UI" don't make sense. If you're asked to test that "intuitive UI" (and, to be clear, you will be in the next step of the canvas,) what will you test? Consider replacing ambiguous phrases like that with more specific ones like "one-click checkout" or "face recognition authentication."

CHAPTER 11

Box 7: What's the Most Important Thing We Need to Learn First?

What's the most important thing we need to learn first?

For each hypothesis from Box 6, identify its riskiest assumptions. Then determine the riskiest one right now. This is the assumption that will cause the entire idea to fail if it's wrong.

(Hint: In the early stages of a hypothesis focus on risks to value rather than feasibility.)

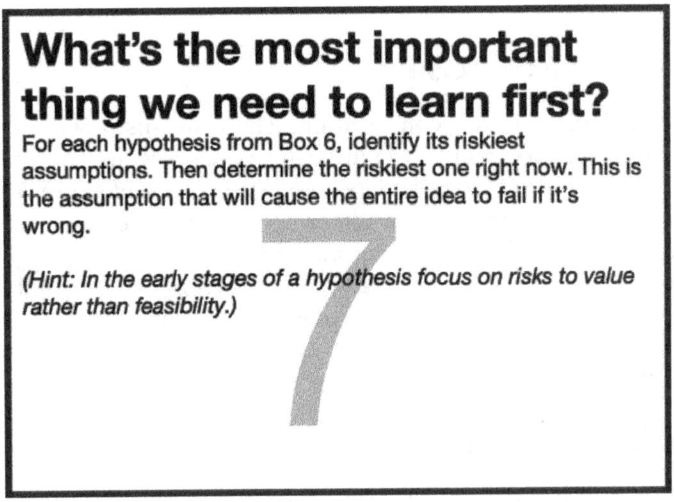

Figure 11-1. *Box 7 of the Lean UX Canvas: Learning*

Once you've prioritized your hypotheses and identified which hypotheses you're going to test, the next step in the process is highlighting the major risks in each hypothesis. To do this, we ask the first of the two key Lean UX questions: *What's the most important thing we need to learn first about this hypothesis?*

When we ask about learning, we're really having a conversation about risk. We want to uncover all the things that might break our hypothesis. If you're doing this with a cross-functional team, as we've advised throughout the book, you're going to get at least as many answers to this question as there are disciplines in the room. The software engineers will discuss the complexities of developing the feature. The designers will bring up workflow issues and usability concerns. Product managers will challenge whether it will deliver the business benefits we anticipate. All of these risks are valid, but the ones we want to focus on now are the ones that will render the hypothesis invalid and allow us to move on quickly if we're wrong.

In the early stages of the hypothesis's life cycle, the biggest risk is usually related to the value of the solution. Do people need a solution? Will they look for it? Will they try it? Will they use it? Will they find value in it? These are the things that matter early on. If the answer to these questions is "no," then there's no need to worry about how we're going to design or build it. If we're dealing with a more mature hypothesis, one where the value has been validated and we've moved on to the technical implementation, then thinking through things like technical challenges, usability, and scalability become the next logical risks to explore.

Facilitating the Exercise

Generally speaking, this is a conversation. The team sits down to review the hypothesis prioritization and determines which ones it wants to test first. Then ask the question *what's the most important thing we need to learn first about this hypothesis?* If the conversation gets stuck, you might choose to brainstorm here, then do some affinity mapping and dot voting. Or you might defer to some member of the team who holds a strong opinion. Generally, this step doesn't need a lot of process. The point here is to identify the top one to three risks related to this hypothesis, then move on to planning your experiment, which you'll do in Box 8.

What to Watch Out For

Consensus is nice but not always attainable. If you find that team discussion not reaching a consensus, it's a clear indication the team needs more information to make that decision. The only way to do that is to make a decision and move forward to Box 8 to create an experiment. In most cases, the product manager can make this call. When you do this, remember that we're not abandoning these hypotheses, assumptions, and risks forever. We're simply moving forward with one and, if proven false, will come back to the backlog of hypotheses to do the process again.

CHAPTER 12

Box 8: MVPs and Experiments

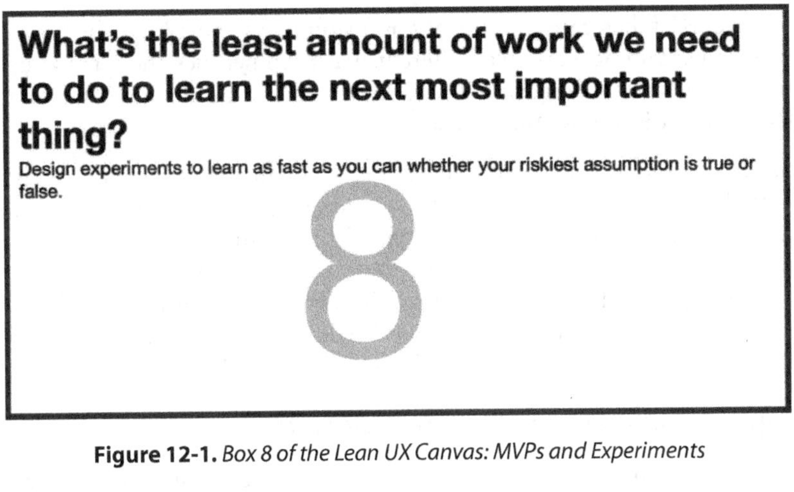

What's the least amount of work we need to do to learn the next most important thing?

Design experiments to learn as fast as you can whether your riskiest assumption is true or false.

Figure 12-1. *Box 8 of the Lean UX Canvas: MVPs and Experiments*

The final step in the Lean UX Canvas is focused on experimentation. The second key question of the canvas we have to answer is *What's the least amount of work we need to do to learn the next most important thing?* The answer to this question is the experiment you're going to run to test your hypothesis.

Doing the least amount of work isn't lazy. It's lean. Remember, we're trying to eliminate waste, and extra work spent testing your idea is waste. In fact, the faster you find out if your idea is something you should continue working on, the less you invest in it. This makes changing course much easier, which increases the agility of the team.

The experiments you come up with in Box 8 are your minimum viable products or MVP. In fact, this is the exact definition of MVP from Eric Ries's *The Lean Startup*.

What Is an MVP Anyway?

If you ask a room full of technology professionals the question "What is an MVP?" you're likely to hear a lengthy and diverse list that includes such gems as the ones that follow:

"It's the fastest thing we can get out the door that still works."

"It's an ugly release that's full of compromises and makes everyone unhappy."

"It's whatever the client says it is."

"It's the minimum set of features that allows us to say, 'it works.'"

"It's phase 1." (And we all know about the likelihood of phase 2.)

The phrase MVP has caused a lot of confusion in its short life. The problem is that it gets used in at least two different ways. Sometimes the term is used to mean "a small and fast release." That's the meaning that the quotes above refer to. That's not how we use the phrase.

When we say MVP, we are talking about a small and fast way of learning something. Sometimes, this is a software release. Sometimes, it's not—it can be a drawing, a landing page, or a prototype. Your primary concern is not to create value but to create learning. Now, these two ideas are not mutually exclusive. After all, one of the key things you're trying to learn is what the market finds valuable. Oftentimes, a good MVP will create both value and learning. For us, though, the point of an MVP is that it's focused on learning.

Example: Should We Launch a Newsletter?

Let's take for example a medium-sized company we consulted with a few years ago. They were exploring new marketing tactics and wanted to launch a monthly newsletter. Creating a successful newsletter is no small task. You need to prepare a content strategy, editorial calendar, layout and design, as well as an ongoing marketing and distribution strategy. You need writers and editors to work on it. All in all, it was a big expenditure for the company to undertake. The team decided to treat this newsletter idea as a hypothesis.

The team asked themselves: *What's the most important thing we need to learn first?* The answer: Was there enough customer demand for a newsletter to justify the effort? The MVP the company used to test the idea was a sign-up form on their current website. The sign-up form promoted the newsletter and asked for a customer's email address. This approach wouldn't deliver any value to the customer—yet. Instead, the goal was to measure demand and build insight on what value proposition and language drove sign-ups. The team felt that these tests would give them enough information to make a good decision about whether to proceed.

The team spent half a day designing and coding the form and was able to launch it that same afternoon. The team knew that their site received a significant amount of traffic each day: they would be able to learn very quickly if there was interest in the newsletter.

At this point, the team made no effort to design or build the actual newsletter. They would do that only after they'd gathered enough data from their first experiment, and only if the data showed that its customers wanted the newsletter. If the data was positive, the team would move on to their next MVP, one that would begin to deliver value and create deeper learning around the type of content, presentation format, frequency, social distribution, and the other things they would need to learn to create a good newsletter. The team planned to continue experimenting with MVP versions of the newsletter—each one improving on its predecessor—that would provide more and different types of content and design, and ultimately deliver the business benefit they were seeking.

Creating an MVP

When it comes to creating an MVP, the first question is always *what is the most important thing we need to learn next?* In most cases, the answer to that will either be a question of value or a question of implementation. In either case, you'll want to design an experiment that provides you with enough evidence to answer your question and help you decide whether or not to continue with the idea.

Creating an MVP to Understand Value

Here are some guidelines to follow if you're trying to understand the value of your idea:

Get to the point
> Regardless of the MVP method you choose to use, focus your time distilling your idea to its core value proposition and present that to your customers. The things that surround your idea (things like navigation, logins, and password retrieval flows) will be irrelevant if your idea itself has no value to your target audience. Leave that stuff for later.

Use a clear call to action

You will know people value your solution when they demonstrate intent to use it or (gasp!) pay for it. Giving people a way to opt in to or sign up for a service is a great way to know if they're interested and whether they'd actually give you money for it.

Measure behavior

Build MVPs with which you can observe and measure what people do. This lets you bypass what people say they (will) do in favor of what they actually do. In digital product design, behavior trumps opinion.

Talk to your users

Measuring behavior tells you what people did with your MVP. Without knowing why they behaved that way, iterating your MVP is an act of random design. Try to capture conversations from both those who converted as well as those who didn't.

Prioritize ruthlessly

Ideas are cheap and plentiful. Let the best ones prove themselves, so don't hold on to invalidated ideas just because you like them. As designers ourselves, we know that this one is particularly difficult to practice. Designers tend to be optimists, and often we believe our solutions, whether we worked on them for five minutes or five months, are well-crafted and properly thought out. Remember, if the results of your experiment disagree with your hypothesis, you're wrong.

Stay agile

Learnings will come in quickly; make sure you're working in a medium or tool that allows you to make updates easily.

Don't reinvent the wheel

Many of the tools, systems, and mechanisms that you need to test your ideas already exist. Consider how you could use email, SMS, chat apps, Facebook Groups, Shopify storefronts, no-code tools, discussion forums, and other existing tools to get the learning you're seeking.

Creating an MVP to Understand Implementation

Here are some guidelines to follow if you're trying to understand the implementation you're considering launching to your customers:

Be functional

Some level of integration with the rest of your application must be in place to create a realistic usage scenario. Creating your new workflow in the context of the existing functionality is important here.

Integrate with existing analytics
    Measuring the performance of your MVP must be done within the context of existing product workflows. This will help you to understand the numbers you're seeing.

Be consistent with the rest of the application
    To minimize any biases toward the new functionality, design your MVP to fit with your current look, feel, and brand.

Some Final Guidelines for Creating MVPs

MVPs might seem simple but in practice can prove challenging. Like most skills, the more you practice, the better you become at doing it. In the meantime, here are some guidelines to building valuable MVPs.

It's not easy to be pure
    You'll find that it's not always possible to test only one thing at a time: you're often trying to learn whether your idea has value and determine implementation details at the same time. Although it's better to separate these processes, keeping the aforementioned guidelines in mind as you plan your MVPs will help you to navigate the trade-offs and compromises you're going to have to make.

Be clear about your learning goals
    Make sure that you know what you're trying to learn, and make sure you are clear about what data you need to collect to learn. It's a bad feeling to launch an experiment only to discover you haven't instrumented correctly and are failing to capture some important data.

Start small
    Regardless of your desired outcome, build the smallest MVP possible. Remember that it is a tool for learning. You will be iterating. You will be modifying it. You might very well be throwing it away entirely. It'll be much easier to throw it away if you didn't spend a lot of time building it.

You don't necessarily need code
    In many cases, your MVP won't involve any code at all. Instead, you will rely on many of the UX designer's existing tools: sketching, prototyping, copywriting, and visual design.

The Truth Curve

The amount of effort you put into your MVP should be proportional to the amount of evidence you have that your idea is a good one. That's the point of the chart (Figure 12-2) created by Giff Constable.[1] The x-axis shows the level of investment you should put into your MVP. The y-axis shows the amount of market-based evidence you have about your idea. The more evidence you have, the higher the fidelity and complexity of your MVP can be. (You'll need the extra effort, because what you need to learn becomes more complex.) The less evidence you have, the less effort you want to put into your MVP. Remember the second key question: *What's the smallest thing that you can do to learn the next most important thing?* Anything more than that is waste.

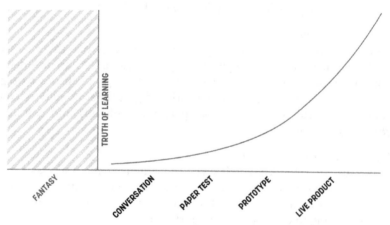

Figure 12-2. *Our adapted version of the Truth Curve is a useful reminder that learning is continuous, and increased investment is only warranted when the facts dictate it*

Examples of MVPs

Let's take a look at a few different types of MVPs that are in common use.

Landing Page Test

This type of MVP helps a team determine demand for their product. It involves creating a marketing page with a clear value proposition, a call to action, and a way to measure conversion. Teams must drive relevant traffic to this landing page to get a large enough sample size for the results to be useful. They can do

---

1 Giff Constable, "The Truth Curve," June 18, 2013, *https://oreil.ly/vAXJ5*.

this either by diverting traffic from existing workflows or utilizing online advertising.

Positive results from landing page tests are clear, but negative results can be difficult to interpret. If no one "converts," it doesn't necessarily mean your idea has no value. It could just mean that you're not telling a compelling story. The good news is that landing page tests are cheap and can be iterated very quickly. If you think about it, Kickstarter (and other crowdfunding sites) are full of landing page MVPs, as demonstrated in Figure 12-3. The people who list products on those sites are looking for validation (in the form of financial backing) that they should invest in actually building their proposed ideas. Landing page tests don't have to be pages. They can be advertisements or other online messages that have the components listed above.

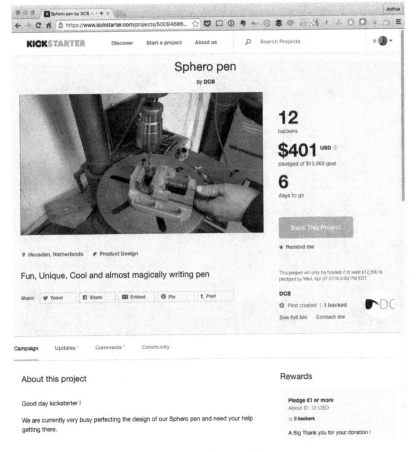

Figure 12-3. *An example of a Kickstarter page*

Feature Fake (aka the Button to Nowhere)

Sometimes, the cost of implementing a feature is very high. In these cases, it is cheaper and faster to create the appearance of the feature where none actually exists. HTML buttons, calls to action, and other prompts and links provide the illusion to your customer that a feature exists. Upon clicking or tapping the link, the user is notified that the feature is "coming soon" and that they will be alerted when this has happened. Feature fakes are like mini-landing pages in that they exist to measure interest. They should be used sparingly and taken down as soon as a success threshold has been reached. If you feel they might negatively affect your relationship with your customer, you can make it right by offering a gift card or some other kind of compensation to those who found your mousetrap.

Figure 12-4 shows a feature fake that Flickr used. In this case, they offered a button labeled "Use as screensaver" that was ostensibly meant for the user to specify a photo album as the screensaver for their device.

Figure 12-4. *An example of a feature fake found in Flickr's Apple TV app*

When users clicked the button, though, they were greeted by the screen shown in Figure 12-5. Flickr used this to gather evidence that a customer would like this feature. By measuring click rates, they could assess demand for this feature before they built it.

Figure 12-5. *The screen that appears after clicking the feature-fake button*

Figure 12-6 presents another feature-fake example. Here, MapMyRun offered the opportunity to take and upload photos while jogging using two modal overlays. No feature existed until they got an indication that a) people wanted this feature and b) how much they'd be willing to pay for it.

Figure 12-6. *Another example of a feature fake, this one on the MapMyRun website*

Wizard of Oz

After you've proven demand for your idea, a Wizard of Oz MVP can help you to figure out the mechanics of your product. This type of MVP looks to the user like a fully functioning digital service. Behind the scenes, though, the data and communication with the initial set of users is handled manually by humans. For example, the team at Amazon behind the Echo ran a Wizard of Oz MVP as part of their initial testing to understand the types of queries people would ask and how quickly they would expect a response. In one room, a user would ask "Alexa" questions, and in another room, a human typed queries into Google, got answers, and replied back. The test users were not aware that they were not using software. The rest of the team was able to observe users and understand how they would use this new product—before significant engineering effort had been invested.

Example: Wizard of Oz MVP for Taproot Plus

In 2014, our company worked with an organization called Taproot Foundation to create an online marketplace for pro bono volunteers. (*Pro bono* is when a professional donates his skills to help a worthy cause. Unlike the unskilled volunteer services many of us participate in on the weekend, pro bono service involves using your professional talents in a volunteer context.)

Our client, Taproot Foundation, had been helping pro bono volunteers and nonprofit organizations find each other for years, but they had always delivered this matching service "by hand," through phone calls, emails, and in-person meetings. Now they wanted to bring that process online: they wanted to create a website that would act as a two-sided marketplace for pro bono volunteers and the organizations that could benefit from their services.

As we started the project, we faced a big set of questions: how should the matching process work? Should the volunteers advertise their services? Should the organizations advertise their projects? What would work better? And after the parties found each other on the website, how should they get started with the project? How should the organizations communicate their needs? How should the volunteers scope the work? Even little details were big questions: how should the parties schedule their first phone call?

We decided this was a perfect time to create a Wizard of Oz MVP. We built a simple website, hand coding just the few static pages that we needed to make it look like we were open for business. We began with about a dozen pages in all: one index page, and then a page for each of the 12 pilot projects we had lined up. Behind the scenes, we had a community manager assemble a list of potential volunteers, and we emailed them, sending them a call to action and a link to our new site. To maintain the illusion that we had a running system, we made sure the email looked like it came from our new system, not from the community manager.

When volunteers clicked the link in the email, they saw our Wizard of Oz site (Figure 12-7). When they used the site to apply for a volunteer opportunity, it looked to them like they were interacting with the system, but behind the scenes, it simply emailed the community manager and team. We tracked all of our interactions in a simple Trello board (Figure 12-8), which served as our "database."

Figure 12-7. *The Wizard of Oz site for Taproot Foundation*

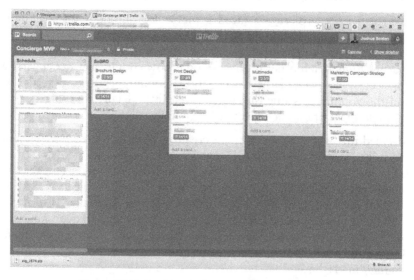

Figure 12-8. *Our "database" was simply a Trello board*

We operated the system this way for a few months, gradually learning from our interactions, updating our business processes, and adding automation and other updates to the website as we learned. Eventually, we added a real functional backend, eliminating much of the "man behind the curtain" aspect of the site. We also updated the visual style, applying some mature graphic design polish (Figure 12-9)—after we had learned enough to understand how to communicate our brand.

Figure 12-9. *The Taproot Plus site with more polished graphic design*

By using a Wizard of Oz approach, we were able to pilot the high-risk parts of the design—the design of the business processes—learn as we went along, and eliminate the risk of spending lots of time and money designing and building the wrong thing.

Prototyping

One of the most effective ways to create MVPs is by prototyping the experience. A prototype is an approximation of an experience that allows you to simulate what it is like to use the product or service in question. It needs to be usable on a variety of target devices. At the same time, your goal should be to spend as little effort as possible in creating the prototype. This makes your choice of prototyping technique important.

Choosing which technique to use for your prototype depends on several factors:

- Who will be interacting with it
- What you hope to learn
- What you already know to be true
- How much time you have to create it

It's critical to define the intended audience for your prototype. This allows you to create the smallest possible prototype that will generate meaningful feedback from this audience. For example, if you're using the prototype primarily to demo ideas to software engineers on your team, you can largely omit primary areas of the product that aren't being affected by the new experience—the global navigation, for example. Your developers know those items are there and that they're not changing, so you don't need to illustrate these items for them.

Stakeholders, often less familiar with their own product than they'll ever admit to, will likely need a greater level of fidelity in the prototype to truly grasp the concept. To meet the various needs of these disparate audiences, your prototyping toolkit should be fairly broad. Let's take a look at the different prototyping techniques and consider when to use each.

Paper Prototypes

Made of the most accessible components—paper, pens, and tape—paper prototypes give you the ability to simulate experiences in a quick, crafty, fun way. No digital investment is necessary. Using tactics like flaps to show and hide different states on a page or even creating a "window" for a slideshow of images to move through, you can begin to give the team a sense of how the product should function. You'll be able to get an immediate sense of what is available in the experience and what is missing. Paper prototyping can give you a sense of how the workflow is starting to coalesce around the interface elements you've assembled. This method is especially helpful with touch interfaces that require the user to manipulate elements on a screen.

Pros

- Can be created in an hour
- Easily arranged and rearranged
- Cheap and easy to throw away if you're wrong
- Can be assembled with materials already found in the office
- Fun activity that many people enjoy

Cons

- Rapid iteration and duplication of the prototype can become time-consuming and tedious.
- The simulation is very artificial, because you're not using the actual input mechanisms (mouse, trackpad, keyboard, touch screen, etc.).
- Feedback is limited to the high-level structure, information architecture, and flow of the product.
- It is only useful with a limited audience.

Low-Fidelity On-Screen Mock-Ups

Creating a low-fidelity clickable on-screen experience—clickable wireframes, for example—lets you take a prototype to the next level of fidelity. Your investment in pixels provides a bit more realistic feel to the workflow. Test participants and team members use digital input mechanisms to interact with the prototype. This lets you get better insight and feedback about the way they will interact with the product at the level of the click, tap, or gesture.

Pros

- Provide a good sense of the length of workflow
- Reveal major obstacles to primary task completion
- Allow assessment of findability of core elements
- Can be used to quickly wire up "something clickable" to get your team learning from your existing assets instead of forcing the creation of new ones

Cons

- Most people who will interact with these assets are savvy enough to recognize an unfinished product.
- More attention than normal is paid to labeling and copy.

Middle- and High-Fidelity On-Screen Prototypes

Middle- and high-fidelity prototypes have significantly more detail than wireframe-based prototypes. You'll use these to demonstrate and test designs that are fleshed out with a level of interaction, visual design, and content that is similar to (or indistinguishable from) the final product experience. The level of interactivity that you can create at this level varies from tool to tool; however, most tools in this category will allow you to represent pixel-perfect simulations of the final experience. You will be able to create interface elements like form fields and drop-down menus that work, and form buttons that simulate submit actions. Some tools allow logical branching and basic data operations. Many allow some types of minor animations, transitions, and state changes.

Pros

- Produce prototypes that are high quality and realistic
- Visual design and brand elements can be tested
- Workflow and user interface interactions can be assessed

Cons

- Interactivity is still more limited than fully native prototypes.
- Users typically can't interact with real data, so there is a limit to the types of product interactions you can simulate.
- Depending on the tool, it can be time-consuming to create and maintain these prototypes. It often creates duplicate effort to maintain a high-fidelity prototype and keep it in sync with the actual product.

No-Code MVP

It's possible to produce a prototype of your product or service that is functional and yet bears no visual resemblance to the final product you have in mind. You do this by making what's come to be called a No-Code MVP. No-Code MVPs rely on the vast array of tools like Airtable, Zapier, and Webflow that require no software development, but still allow you to wire together a service that delivers functionality and, hopefully, some value to customers and end users.

Pros

- Provides a rapid way to test functionality before writing custom software
- Helps you focus on the unique and differentiating parts of your service, without wasting time on building lots of infrastructure
- Requires little to no software development skills

Cons

- Hard to represent brand, graphic design, and other finer points of the presentation
- Hard to maintain over time
- Cheap to get started but expensive to scale

Coded and Live-Data Prototypes

Coded prototypes offer up the highest level of fidelity for simulated experiences. For all intents and purposes, people interacting with this type of prototype should not be able to distinguish it from the final product unless they bump up against the limits of its scope (i.e., they click a link to a page that was not prototyped). Coded prototypes typically exist in the native environment (the browser, the OS, on the device, etc.) and make use of all of the expected interactive elements. Buttons, drop-down menus, and form fields all function as the user would expect. They take input from the mouse, keyboard, and screen. They create as natural an interaction pattern as possible for the prototype's evaluators.

In terms of prototyping with data, there are two levels of fidelity here: hardcoded (or static data) and live data. The hardcoded prototypes look and function like the end product but don't handle real data input, processing, or output. They are still just simulations and typically illustrate a few predefined scenarios. The live-data prototypes will connect with real data, process user input, and show appropriate data outputs. These are often deployed to real customers and offer a level of realism to customers and insight into the customers' use of the prototype that are not available from hardcoded prototypes. You also can use them when A/B testing (that is, comparing two versions of a feature to see which performs better) certain features or changes to the current workflow.

Pros

- Potential to reuse code for production
- The most realistic simulation to create
- Can be generated from existing code assets

Cons

- The team can become bogged down in debating the finer points of the prototype.
- It's time-consuming to create working code that delivers the desired experience.
- It's tempting to perfect the code before releasing to customers.
- Updating and iterating can take a lot of time.

What Should Go into My Prototype?

You've picked the tool to create your MVP and are ready to begin. There is no need to prototype the entire product experience. Focus on the core workflows that let you test the biggest risks in your hypothesis.

Focusing on the primary workflows when you create your MVP gives the team a sense of temporary tunnel vision (in a good way!), allowing them to focus on a specific portion of the experience and assess its validity and efficacy.

Demos and Previews

You might have developed your MVP with a focus on just one kind of user or just one segment of your customer base, but you can learn a lot by sharing your work with your colleagues. Test your prototyped MVP with your team-mates, stakeholders, and members of other teams. Take it to the lunch area and share it with some colleagues who work on different projects. Ensure that, internally, people are providing the team with insights into how well it works, how they'll use it, and whether or not it's worth investing in further. Let stakeholders click through it and give you their insights and thoughts.

If your team has a demo day (and if they don't, they should), bring the prototype there to show progress on the project. The more exposure the MVP receives, the more insight you'll have as to its validity. Next, take your prototype to customers and potential customers. Let them click through the experience and collect their feedback.

Example: Using a Prototype MVP

Let's see how one team we recently worked with used a prototype MVP. In this case study, the team was considering making a significant change to their offering. We used a prototype MVP to support the research and decision-making process.

This established startup was struggling with their current product—an exclusive subscription-based community for group collaboration. It had been in market for a few years and had some initial traction, but adoption had reached a plateau—new users were not signing up. What's more, the product was facing growing competition. Realizing that a radical change was in order, the team considered revamping their business model and opening up the product to a significantly broader market segment. Their concern was two-fold:

1. Would current users accept this change, given that it would alter the exclusive nature of the community?

2. Would the new market segment even be interested in this type of product?

The team was worried that they could take a double hit. They feared that existing users would abandon the product and that there wouldn't be enough new users coming on board to make up for the shortfall.

We worked with the team to define our plan as a hypothesis. We laid out the new market segment and defined the core set of functionality that we wanted to offer to them. This was a subset of the ultimate vision, but it could be demonstrated in five wireframes.

We spent a week creating the wireframes to ensure that our developers, marketers, and executives were committed to the new direction. We showed the wireframes to current customers, getting two rounds of customer feedback over the course of these five days, and we ended up with a clickable prototype —our MVP.

The timing for our experiment was fortuitous: there was a conference full of potential customers scheduled for the following week in Texas. The team went to the conference and walked the halls of the convention center with the prototype on our iPads.

The mock-ups worked great on the iPads: customers tapped, swiped, and chatted with us about the new offering. Three days later, we returned to New York City with feedback written on every sticky note and scrap of paper we could find.

We sorted the notes into groups, and some clear themes emerged. Customer feedback let us conclude that although there was merit to this new business plan, we would need further differentiation from existing products in the marketplace if we were going to succeed.

All told, we spent eight business days developing our hypotheses, creating our MVP, and getting market feedback. This put us in a great position to pivot our position and refine the product to fit our market segment more effectively.

CHAPTER 13

Bringing It All Together

In this section, we've laid out all of the major techniques in Lean UX, from framing your work as a business problem statement to defining success in terms of outcomes for both the business and the user. We've shown you how to capture the essence of what you know about your users as proto-personas. We've talked about how to get started figuring out your solutions. And we've shared ways to write and test your hypotheses. The Lean UX Canvas gives you a concise, single-page way to organize your work as you apply these techniques in the real world.

That said, the real world is a messy place, and every project you work on will be messy in its own way. (That's one of the reasons to use the canvas in the first place!) To wrap up this section, we thought we'd share some stories of teams using Lean UX in this very messy real world. You'll see how well Lean UX works—in fact, how well-suited it is to addressing the messiness of the real world.

In these stories, you'll see that some of these teams used the canvas. Others just used some of the Lean UX techniques that are embedded in the canvas, without using the canvas itself to organize their work. As we've said before, this is fine. Take these tools and make them your own. We hope these stories will give you some ideas and inspiration for how to do just that.

The Lean UX Canvas in the Enterprise

Recently we heard from a product and design leader at a large enterprise software company in Silicon Valley. This company develops a cloud computing platform to help companies manage digital workflows for enterprise operations. They got in touch because they wanted to tell us how they'd been using the Lean UX canvas to kick off projects and new initiatives. We thought it was a great story to share.

A team at this company was working on the second release of a product that had received good feedback from customers. The product had a novel way of displaying data—a display that was really beautiful, that tested well, and that generated really positive feedback from customers. The product used an unusual UI element: a custom-built map that helped users visualize work processes and spot opportunities for process improvements.

In addition to generating positive feedback from customers, this UI showed really well internally. Stakeholders loved it and supported the idea of enhancing it. So it seemed like a natural choice to build on the success of this feature in the next version, and, in fact, that's what the team planned to do: they were going to really lean into this feature for the second release.

Still, they had recently come across the Lean UX Canvas as a tool and liked the way that it spurred methodical thinking about the work they needed to do. They decided to work through a Lean UX Canvas for this initiative. When they did, an interesting thing happened. When they came to Chapter 8, they had a breakthrough.

In order to complete Box 4, the team had to turn back to the feedback data that they had already collected from customers. This often happens when you work on a Lean UX Canvas: you have to find the information that you need to complete a section. Sometimes that means you need to do additional research, and sometimes it simply means you have to review the research you've already done.

In this case, as the team reviewed their data, they noticed an important pattern in the user feedback they'd overlooked: customers were telling them they loved the map, but they wanted more from the product than simply data display. They wanted the product to be more proactive. They were saying essentially, "The display is really beautiful, but we want you to highlight where we should be paying attention."

The process of completing a Lean UX Canvas forced the team to stop and methodically examine the data they had collected. One team member told me, "We actually had the feedback. We just weren't listening to it!" He continued: "When we used the canvas to go through the data about what was materially important to our customers, we realized that we had simply been ignoring the data!"

So the team spent time interpreting this feedback. They really dug in and worked out what they thought the feedback meant and what it meant about the outcomes customers were seeking. When they went back to the customers to validate these ideas, customers responded positively.

After that, the team made an easy decision: they needed to change their priorities. One team member told us that the conversation on the team was clear. "When the voting came down, it wasn't 'make the map better'; it was 'let's do what our customers really find valuable.'"

In the pilot for the second release, "we got really high marks from our customers." Those high marks helped the team get to broad release even faster. "We probably got there six months sooner because of this feedback."

Validately: Validating Your Product with Customer Interviews and a Two-Day Prototype

Serial entrepreneur Steven Cohn got the idea to launch Validately because of the challenges he faced as an entrepreneur doing his own user research. When he surveyed the landscape, he discovered that other user researchers had similar challenges. User researchers were typically using free tools like Skype and Google Docs to conduct their studies. He knew that these tools weren't designed for user research and made the process inefficient. Some teams supplemented these tools with the best-known service provider in the space, usertesting.com. He knew that there was an opportunity here.

Steven and his team used customer interviews to discover this user's needs and goals (Box 4 of the Lean UX Canvas). In these conversations, they discovered where they should focus when they asked researchers what they do with the results their studies generated. "That's where the bulk of my work is," they told him. In fact, he learned that the bulk of researchers' work began once the actual research was over.

The Validately team learned that, following a round of customer interviews or usability tests, researchers had to go back to a lengthy and disorganized Google Doc of notes and connect those notes to timestamps in the video of the study. They would use these timestamps (and some kind of video editing tool) to create video clips, assemble these clips into a highlight reel, and finally share that reel with their teams, clients, and stakeholders. All this just to share what they learned during the study.

The team conducted dozens of interviews to validate this problem. They learned that this work—creating reports and video highlights—was frequently more than 50% of the total effort devoted to each study. He knew he'd found a problem worth solving.

The next step was to work on the solution. (Box 5 of the Lean UX Canvas.) Steven and team created a prototype in InVision that hypothesized what a streamlined tool that combined note taking, time tracking, and report and highlight reel creation could look like. They spent two days creating this prototype before showing it to customers.

The prototype almost single-handedly answered the question "How are you better than usertesting.com?" Once potential customers saw the value of the streamlined tool Validately wanted to build, they were immediately interested. At this point, Steven and team asked for one more type of "feedback." They asked people to commit on the spot—to purchasing a product not in the future but right now, even though it wasn't ready for delivery. The contract offered a cancelation clause if delivery didn't happen, but otherwise, Steven used the prototype as a selling tool for a service that did not yet exist. The pitch worked, which helped Validately validate that their solution was the right one. They converted enough customers to build a thriving business in the gaps between free tools like Google Docs and Skype. Validately went on to be a huge success, ultimately selling to UserZoom in 2019.

The MVPs they used here—customer conversation followed by a two-day prototype—helped Steven and team gather three levels of validation:

Time

> Will people give us 30 minutes of their time to discuss this problem? If not, the problem we're solving is not important enough to them and likely not a space we want to play in.

Social

> Will the people we speak with take it to their boss, team, infosec, procurement, and others in the organization? Will they socialize it and endorse it internally? To understand this, they always asked, "Will you introduce me to others in the organization who might be interested in this tool?" Again, if this resulted in no introductions, that was also a signal.

Money

> If the prospective customer gave their time and their reputation, they'd be asked to purchase. This is the ultimate validation as it actually resulted in a sale.

Kaplan Test Prep: Using Lean UX to Launch a New Business

Kaplan Test Prep has been helping students in the US prepare for standardized tests like college and medical school entrance exams since 1938. Now, with education transforming on a nearly annual basis, Kaplan has to continuously reinvent how it delivers value to its customers. Lee Weiss, currently a senior vice president at the company, has helped Kaplan do exactly this for more than 20 years. Most recently, in the fall of 2018, Lee started thinking about a new idea to reinvent Kaplan's university partnerships business. He wanted to make it possible for universities to create online courses for high school students on the topics of college and career readiness.

Their idea was to create a safe way for high school students to learn about various career paths and try out different universities at the same time. Lee and his colleagues spent a few weeks sketching out some ideas of how this could work and put their thoughts down in a PowerPoint deck. This deck became their first experiment—their MVP—to help them test their first hypothesis: that leadership would be interested in their plans.

In early 2019, they met with the leadership team to test their idea. Kaplan's leaders were excited about this new idea and gave Lee and his colleague Liz Laub the green light to focus solely on this new idea. Kaplan's leadership team told Lee and Liz, "Take the next 90 days and see if you can get this concept off the ground."

Lee and Liz started by asking themselves the first key question of Lean UX: What's the most important thing we need to learn first? (Box 7 on the Lean UX Canvas.)

They realized they wouldn't have a business at all if they couldn't get any universities interested. With their biggest risk identified, they were able to move on to the second key Lean UX question: What's the least amount of work we need to do to learn it? (Box 8 on the Lean UX Canvas.)

They started talking to universities to see if they'd be interested in partnering with them on this initiative—even though the initiative itself did not yet exist. Within 90 days, the team had spoken to 20 different universities and ended up with 2 of the biggest universities in the US interested in the idea—all through simple, and at times serendipitous, conversation. This was great news, as it would give Lee and Liz enough information to make a more detailed request from leadership. A request for budget to bring a product to market.

Before they could do that, though, there were other questions they'd need to answer: like what would students and parents want? What would their solution look like? (These are the kinds of questions you capture in Box 7 of the canvas.)

This is where the obstacles started to appear: their assumptions about their product offering (Chapter 9) started getting smashed on the rocks of reality. Initially, they'd hoped to build a product that allowed teachers and students to interact together in real time. Unfortunately, time zones got in the way of that, something they learned quickly through early and continuous conversations with students. So they pivoted to asynchronous courses and quickly faced a new challenge: how to build an engaging and high-value course.

They assumed that the best way to do this would be to build cohort-based communities. They tested their assumptions by starting to create early versions of this offering. While this received strong positive feedback from the students who were involved in the tests, there was still demand from both parents and students for live mentoring and support. They addressed this by hiring former students from these universities as mentors. These pieces were the foundations of a product that met both synchronous and asynchronous needs.

There was one last piece of the puzzle they had to explore in their initial 90-day period, though: their hypotheses about the kind of organization they would need to build and support this business. It wouldn't do them any good to solve this need in the market with a compelling product if they couldn't create a viable, sustainable business. (These service-design considerations should be part of your solution definition in Box 5.)

Here again the team made a series of assumptions about who they'd need to hire, how they should price the product, how much it would cost to run it, and, of course, what shape the product should take. Lee notes that nearly all of these assumptions were wrong in hindsight, but they now had enough information to go back to leadership with a more detailed request: a request for budget—$700,000 to be exact—to get the product built and to market. The request was approved, with one caveat: you have one year to break even.

The team got started. Using nothing more than conversations with students, teachers, and administrators at their two (now signed) customers, the team created an initial curriculum of three courses. The goal was to make the highest quality courses they could as quickly as possible.

With the curriculum in place, the team needed operational systems to support the work—CRM, learning management systems, content management systems, etc. They sought systems with the mandate to use whatever got them up and running the fastest. They stitched together a lightweight experience using SaaS products—all outside the Kaplan tech ecosystem, which would have slowed down their ability to run quick tests. (This is a great use of the No-Code MVP technique.)

The first two-week course had eight students in it, all of whom got the course for free. All eight finished the course and gave strong positive feedback about the product quality and overall experience. Now it was time to acquire the first paid cohort. There wasn't a lot of interest at first. Lee, Liz, and the team were starting to worry. Their application was long, the cost was high, and the $50 application fee they'd seen elsewhere and copied into their product all seemed to be keeping potential customers from submitting their applications.

The next experiments were clear to the team—remove the application fee, shorten the application process, and lower the price. They were able to do this for two reasons. First, because they were an internal innovation team, they had decision-making authority to explore pricing. So they cut their prices in half. The second reason that they could experiment like this? They were working in one-week sprints. So even if a decision was catastrophic, the longest they had to live with it was one week.

The team didn't have to wait long, though. The day they made the changes, they got more applications than the prior two weeks combined. Sales revenue quintupled. As the product saw stronger traction, the team began to worry about maintaining product quality as they scaled. They defined a set of outcome-based metrics to guide their decision making and keep quality high: they wanted to make sure that every student logged in within 48 hours of any course starting, they wanted to see an 80% course completion rate, and they wanted to maintain a Net Promoter Score (NPS) of 50.

By using outcomes as their north stars, evidence-based decision making as their engine, and short cycles to keep themselves on track, the team has managed to build a business unit that now employs more than 30. They proved that following data and instinct and slowly scaling up decisions allows you to make the best course corrections along the way. When you couple this data with an autonomous team and a clear, outcome-based mandate, the results speak for themselves.

PART III

COLLABORATION

It's Tuesday, and Rick, Mark, Olga, and Arti are standing at the whiteboard, looking at a wireframe that they've drawn. Arti, the designer, has a marker in her hand, but she's not drawing. "Rick, I don't understand what you're driving at. Can you explain the problem?" she asks.

Rick takes the marker, wipes clear a section of the board, and explains the regulation, again. The team is designing an app for stock traders, and the app must obey a strict set of regulations. Rick, the business analyst, is responsible for making sure that the team's designs support the rules.

After a while, the team is nodding, and Arti takes the marker again. She suggests a change to the wireframe design of the app on the board, and the team nods again. They all take out their iPhones, take photos of the board, and agree to reconvene the next day. They're confident that what they've agreed on will be ready for user testing on Thursday.

Arti goes back to her desk to begin detailing out the design they've sketched. Mark, the frontend developer, begins building the page—he uses components from the Design System the team has built, so he doesn't need to wait for Arti before getting the basic pieces in place. Rick opens the project's wiki page and begins to document the decisions the team has made about the application's behavior. He'll review these choices with the product owner later in the day.

And Olga, the QA tester, begins the process of writing tests for the new section of the app.

This is the day-to-day rhythm of Lean UX: a team working collaboratively, iteratively, and in parallel, with few handoffs, minimal deliverables, and a focus on working software and market feedback. In this section, you'll see how it's done.

About Part III

In the previous part, we looked at the Lean UX Canvas, the tool that we use to organize our Lean UX process. We also looked at the various tools within the Lean UX process. In this section, we'll look at another dimension of Lean UX: the way we work together with our users, customers, stakeholders, and colleagues.

The Lean UX Process

Chapter 14, "Collaborative Design", is about one of the major elements of Lean UX—the way it encourages cross-functional collaboration. It encourages designers to work with their nondesign colleagues to create the best possible products. This chapter will talk about some of the most important ways that we do that.

Chapter 15, "Feedback and Research", is about how Lean UX advocates continuous research and collaborative research. This can feel like a change for a lot of teams, so we discuss some of the key things you'll need to know here.

Chapter 16, "Integrating Lean UX and Agile", is all about how Lean UX and Agile methods work together. Agile is one of the foundational pillars of Lean UX. Lean UX was born from a need to work with Agile software development teams—a struggle many designers face on a daily basis. This chapter will help you navigate.

CHAPTER 14

Collaborative Design

Be open to collaboration. Other people and other people's ideas are often better than your own. Find a group of people who challenge and inspire you, spend a lot of time with them, and it will change your life.

Amy Poehler

What is a "user experience"? It's the sum total of all of the interactions a user has with your product and service. It's created by all of the decisions that you and your team make about your product or service: the way you price it, the way you package and sell it, the way you onboard users, the way you support it and maintain it and upgrade it, and so on and so on. In other words, it's created by a team, not an individual designer. For this reason, Lean UX begins with the idea that user experience design should be a collaborative process.

Lean UX brings designers and nondesigners together in cocreation. It yields ideas that are bigger and better than their individual contributors. To be clear, though, we're not advocating "design by committee," a phrase that implies a process filled with bad compromises and uninformed decision making. Instead, Lean UX processes are orchestrated and facilitated by designers and executed by discipline specialists working from a common playbook. Lean UX increases your team's ownership over the work by providing an opportunity for individual points of view to be shared early and continuously through the process. Ultimately, it's about using the diverse expertise of your team to create designs that *work*.

In this chapter we'll explore the many benefits that come from this close, cross-functional collaboration.

Let's dig in...

Collaborative Design

In Chapter 10, you learned about hypotheses. To test your hypotheses, you sometimes simply conduct research (described in Chapter 12). But other times, you need to design and build something that will help you to test these hypotheses. For example, if you're in the early stage of a project, you might test demand by creating a landing page that will measure how many customers sign up for your service. Or if you're later in the product life cycle, you might be working at the feature level—adding some new functionality that will make users more productive, for example. Navigating the many possible design options for these features can be difficult for teams. How often have you experienced team conflict over design choices?

The most effective way we've found to rally a team around a design direction is through collaboration. Over the long haul, collaboration yields better results than hero-based design (the practice of calling in a designer or design team to drop in, come up with something beautiful, and take off to rescue the next project). Teams rarely learn or get better from working with heroes. Instead, in the same way that creating hypotheses together increases the product IQ of the team, designing together increases the design IQ of the team. It allows all of the members of the team to articulate their ideas. It gives designers a much broader set of ideas to draw upon as they refine the design. This, in turn, increases the entire team's feelings of ownership in the work. Finally, collaborative design builds team-wide shared understanding. It is this shared understanding that is the currency of Lean UX. The more the team collectively understands, the less it has to document in order to move forward.

Collaborative design is an approach that allows a team to design together. It helps teams build a shared understanding of both the design problem and the solution. It provides the means for them to work together to decide which functionality and interface elements best implement the feature they want to create.

Collaborative design is still a designer-led activity. It's the designer's responsibility to not only call collaborative design meetings but facilitate them as well. Sometimes, you'll have informal chats and sketching sessions. Sometimes, more structured one-on-one sessions with a developer at a whiteboard. Other times, you will gather the entire team for a Design Studio exercise or even a Design Sprint. The key is to collaborate with a diverse group of team members.

In a typical collaborative design session, teams sketch together, critique the work as it emerges, and ultimately converge on a solution they feel has the greatest chance of success. The designer, while still producing designs, takes on the additional role of facilitator to lead the team through a series of exercises.

The output of these sessions typically consists of low-fidelity sketches and wireframes. This level of fidelity is important. First, it makes it possible for everyone to contribute, even team members with less sophisticated drawing skills. Second, it's critical to maintaining the malleability of the work. This gives the team the ability to pivot quickly if their tests reveal that the approach isn't working. It's much easier to pivot from a failed approach if you haven't spent too much time laboriously drawing, documenting, and detailing that approach.

Collaborative Design: The Informal Approach

A few years ago, Jeff was designing a dashboard for a web app targeted at TheLadders' recruiter and employer audience. There was a lot of information to fit on one screen, and he was struggling to make it all work. Instead of burning too much time at his desk pushing pixels, he grabbed a whiteboard and asked Greg, the lead developer, to join him. Jeff sketched his original idea about how to lay out all of the content and functionality for this dashboard (see Figure 14-1). The two of them then discussed the idea, and eventually Jeff handed Greg the marker. He sketched his ideas on the same whiteboard. They went back and forth, ultimately converging on a layout and flow they felt was both usable and feasible, given that they needed to deliver a solution within the current two-week sprint. At the end of that two-hour session, they returned to their desks and began working. Jeff refined the sketch into a more formal wireframe and workflow, while Greg began to write the infrastructure code necessary to get the data they needed to the presentation layer.

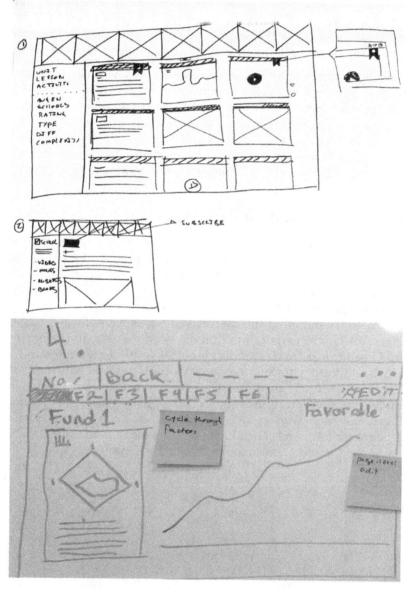

Figure 14-1. *Examples of whiteboard sketches*

They had built a shared understanding through their collaborative design session. They both knew what they were going to build and what the feature needed to do. They didn't need to wait to document it. This allowed them to get the first version of this idea built within a two-week time frame.

Conversation: Your Most Powerful Tool

Lean UX promotes conversation as the primary means of communication among team members. In this way, it is very much in line with the Agile Manifesto, which promotes "individuals and interactions over processes and tools." Conversation unites a team around a shared vision. It also brings insights from different disciplines to the project much earlier than a traditional design cycle would allow. As new ideas are formed or changes are made to the design, a team member's insight can quickly challenge those changes in a way the designer alone wouldn't have recognized.

By having these conversations early and often, the team is aware of everyone's ideas and can get started on their own work earlier. If they know that the proposed solution requires a certain backend infrastructure, for example, the team's engineers can get started on that work while the design is refined and finalized. Parallel paths for software development and design are the fastest route to reach an actual experience.

These conversations might seem awkward at first; after all, you're breaking down time-tested walls between disciplines. As the conversation evolves, however, designers provide developers with input on the implementation of certain features, ensuring the proper evolution of their vision. These conversations promote transparency of process and progress. This transparency builds a common language and deeper bonds between team members. Teammates who trust one another are more motivated to work together to produce higher-quality work.

Find ways to have more conversations with your teammates, both work-related and not. Time spent cultivating social ties with your team—eating meals together, for example—can make work-related conversations easier, more honest, and more productive.

Lean UX and Design Sprints

In Chapter 9, we wrote about an exercise called "Design Studio." This is a great way to gather a team for a structured design session. In recent years, a similar approach called "Design Sprint" has become popular. Described in the book *Sprint* by Jake Knapp, John Zeratsky, and Braden Kowitz (Simon and Schuster), a design sprint is a five-day process that gathers a team, defines a question, develops ideas, builds a prototype, and tests it—all in a single week. Design Sprints are like a Design Studio on steroids. Or like a mini-cycle of Lean UX work. Having now facilitated a few of our own, we've seen how powerful this process can be. If you're looking to kick-start a team, a project, or an initiative, a Design Sprint is a great way to go.[1]

That said, there are some perhaps contradictory parts of the methods. Lean UX has a particular way to frame problems, for example. Design Sprints frame problems on day one using a different method. Lean UX recommends hypotheses, experiments, and MVPs to test your ideas. Design Sprints take teams through prototyping and testing during the final days of the sprint in a way that doesn't use hypotheses or the word MVP. So sometimes it feels like the methods are in conflict.

Our perspective is that the methods are deeply compatible in spirit, if not in exact practice. If you can embrace the spirit of the methods, Design Sprints fit really well into a Lean UX approach.

That said, we wanted to learn a little more, so we reached out to Jake Knapp to talk through some of our questions.

Lean UX and Design Sprints: A Conversation with Jeff, Josh, and Jake Knapp

Q: Lots of people have questions about how Lean UX and Design Sprints work together. Do you have POV on this question?

Jake Knapp: To me, Lean UX is like a cookbook you can use across your entire product cycle and throughout your entire organization. Design Sprints are a single recipe—something very specific for a specific moment with a specific part of your team. The philosophies are totally compatible. Anyone who is familiar with Lean UX should check out Design Sprints, and vice versa.

Q: How much flexibility is there in the Design Sprint recipe? Can we adjust the recipe?

JK: Yes...but don't adjust the recipe until you've tried the original. The steps are in there for a reason, and they work, but if you've run Design Sprints by the book a few times and you think you need an adjustment, try it!

Q: That's great to hear—because that's how we recommend people think about Lean UX. It's always a matter of trying things, learning, and adjusting based on what you've learned.

JK: That's right. Observe what happens and take notes. Treat it like an experiment within the experiment. And if you find an improvement, please let me know.

Q: What are Design Sprints really great at? What are they not great for?

---

1 The word "sprint" can be confusing here. In this context, we're not talking about an Agile-style sprint, what Scrum would call an "iteration." When we use the phrase "Design Sprint," we'll use capital letters to indicate that we're talking about the specific process described in the book *Sprint*.

JK: Design Sprints are great for teams who want to build something new or shake things up. They're ideal for starting big projects and improving your hunch about product/market fit. They're great for building momentum and alignment on a team...in other words, a Design Sprint gets everybody rowing in the same direction with a real purpose. They're also great at resetting team culture and encouraging the best kind of risk-taking and decision making. They can bring people a better understanding of and focus on their customers, and they can bring people closer to their colleagues. They can bring a renewed sense of joy in work, because you finally get to cut through all the baloney and just do what matters most.

Q: OK, now the other side of that question: What are they NOT great for?

JK: Design Sprints are NOT meant for designing every detail of your product or planning out your entire development schedule. They don't replace your MVP, and they don't offer you a path from zero to launch. They're really good at this one specific moment—in fact, I can confidently say they are the best way I know of to start a new project. Before and after that moment...well, refer to the rest of the book you're holding. :)

Q: There seems to be a lot of overlap between the methods. Which one should we do?

JK: Both!

Using Design Sprints in a Lean UX Process

So, as you can see from our conversation with Jake, we all believe the methods work well together. So, then, what is the best way to use Lean UX to set up a successful Design Sprint? And how can you use Lean UX after you've run a Design Sprint?

Here's what we recommend:

- Remember that Lean UX encourages you to reframe your work as a problem to solve rather than a "thing to build." Don't go into a sprint thinking, "What can we build?" Instead, use your sprint to figure out "How can we solve our problem?"
- Lean UX encourages you to articulate your assumptions about the problem, the target audience, potential solutions, and what success looks like. This allows you to frame hypotheses, which can be a great way to frame a design sprint.
- Use your hypothesis(es) as input to your Design Sprint.
- Use the work you do in the sprint to start to tear apart these assumptions, test them, and come out the other end with a better set of hypotheses and a clear set of next steps.

- This next set of hypotheses can be used as input to your next cycle of Lean UX work.

Design Systems

As the story of Jeff and Greg at the whiteboard makes clear, collaborative design is most effective when you're working with what we think of as a fat pen. Design Sprints are another technique that embraces this fat-pen way of working. You're sketching together, making high-level decisions about concept, structure, flow, and functionality. This is the level of resolution and detail that is most appropriate for collaborative design. Collaborative design almost never means that teams are sitting together at a workstation moving pixels around. In fact, this kind of group hovering at the pixel level is what most designers would consider their worst nightmare. (To be clear: *don't do this.*)

And yet, design isn't done when the sketch is done. It's not completed on the whiteboard. Instead, it's usually just getting started. So how do we get design to the pixel level? How do we get to finished visual design?

Increasingly, we're seeing teams turn to design systems. Design systems are like style guides on steroids. When we wrote the first edition of this book, design systems were a new thing. In fact, as an industry, we hadn't really decided yet what to call them. Back then, we were excited about design systems because they promised to unlock collaboration between designers and developers, and to solve once many of the repetitive and rote problems that designers faced, which meant that designers could move on to the tougher challenges that added more value.

By the time we wrote the second edition of this book, four years later, design systems had gone mainstream. Forward-thinking large organizations had built or were building their enterprise-scale systems. Startups were putting them in place from day one. Consulting organizations that specialized in design systems had sprung up. Conferences were bringing practitioners together. We had many more examples that we could feature in the second edition of the book, and we've left them in place for your reference.

Fast-forward to today. Design systems are now a well-established part of the way design gets done in our industry. They continue to deliver on the promise of the early days—including the benefits we were so excited about when we first encountered them: they continue to allow product teams to work in collaborative and highly agile ways. Before we get into some of the ways that design systems help teams be more agile, let's take a look at what they are.

Design Systems: What's in a Name?

Style guides. Pattern libraries. Brand guidelines. Asset libraries. Design systems. There's not a lot of common language in this part of the design world, so let's take a moment to clarify our terms.

For years, large organizations created brand guidelines (Figure 14-2)—comprehensive documents of brand design and usage rules for those companies. In predigital days, these guidelines were documents, sometimes a few pages, but frequently large, comprehensive bound volumes. As the world moved online, these books sometimes moved onto the web as PDF documents, web pages, or even wikis.

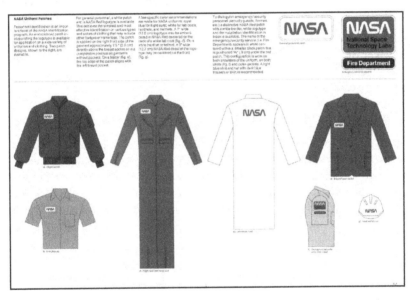

Figure 14-2. *Example of brand standards guidelines, this one from NASA[2]*

At the same time, publishers and publications often maintained style guides that covered rules of writing and content presentation. College students in the United States are familiar with the comforting strictness of *The Chicago Manual of Style*, *The MLA Style Manual and Guide to Scholarly Publishing*, and others.

The computing world's version of a style guide is exemplified by Apple's famous Human Interface Guidelines (HIG). The HIG is a comprehensive

2 NASA, "NASA Graphics Standards Manual," September 8, 2015, *https://oreil.ly/nCc4H*.

document that explains every component in Apple's operating system, provides rules for using the components, and contains examples that demonstrate proper use of the components.

Finally, developers are familiar with *asset libraries*. These collections of reusable code elements are intended to make the developer's job easier by providing tested, reusable code that's easy to download from an always current *code repository*.

As with many ideas in the digital world, digital design systems (which we'll call design systems for the sake of brevity) are a kind of mash-up of all of these ideas. A good design system contains comprehensive documentation of the elements of a design, rules and examples that govern the use of these elements, and, crucially, *the code and other assets that actually implement the design*.

In practice, a design system functions as a single source of truth for the presentation layer of a product. Teams can sketch at the whiteboard and then quickly use the elements found in the design system to assemble a prototype or production-ready frontend.

The Value of Design Systems

Design systems are a powerful enabler of Lean UX. They allow the visual and microinteraction details of a design to be developed and maintained in parallel with the other decisions a team makes. So decisions like screen structure, process flow, information hierarchy—things that can be worked out at the whiteboard—can be handled by the right group of teammates, whereas things like color, type, and spacing can be handled by another (very likely overlapping) group of folks.

This has a couple of big benefits for teams:

Design faster
    The team isn't reinventing the wheel every time they design a screen.

Prototype faster
    Frontend developers are working from a kit of parts—they don't need to recreate the elements of a solution each time; they can just go get the appropriate pieces out of the design system.

It also has some big benefits for organizations:

Increased consistency
    A good design system is easy for developers to use. So they are more likely to use parts that they find in the design system and less likely to "roll their own." This means a greater likelihood that their work will adhere to brand standards.

Increased quality

By centralizing the design and creation of user-facing elements, you can take advantage of the work of a few highly trained and highly specialized designers and UI developers. Their high-quality work can be implemented by other less-specialized developers in the organization to produce top-notch results.

Lower costs

A good design system is not free. It requires investment to build it and staff to maintain it. But over time, it pays for itself by providing tools and frameworks that make the users of the system—the other developers in the organization—more efficient and more productive. It allows new designers to come up to speed more quickly, for example, because it documents all of the frontend conventions used in an app. Similarly, it allows new developers to come up to speed more quickly, because the basic building blocks of their work are available in an easy-to-use framework.

Design Systems Teams Are Product Teams

Make no mistake: a design systems team is a product team. Though this team is working on a product that will be used (in most cases) by internal users, this team is nevertheless a product team. It will have many of the same concerns that any product team will have: first and foremost, it needs to make a product that its users find valuable. As with any internal product, your measure of success is not sales; it's *adoption*. So understanding the needs of your users and serving them will be key to rapid adoption of your work and, ultimately, key to your success.

Design systems teams can approach this challenge using Lean UX methods. Some methods, like certain kinds of experimentation, can be difficult or impossible for design systems teams: because design systems are platform products, they will be used by teams in a variety of contexts and must integrate into a wide range of environments. So compatibility and stability concerns can limit the kinds of experiments you run.

That said, because the users of design systems are internal, you should have an easy time getting access to them. This means that design systems teams can lean into the techniques of collaborative design, using workshops, sprints, and shared whiteboard sessions to build collaboration and shared understanding between design systems developers and users.

Don't Skip the Fat Markers

One surprising concern that we've seen as design systems become more ubiquitous is that design systems can be so good and so easy to use that designers can be tempted to skip right past the "fat marker" stage of design and go right to high-fidelity work. When this happens, artifacts that represent early-stage thinking—the concept development stage of the work—can sometimes be misunderstood by stakeholders, colleagues, and even the designers themselves. It's human nature to respond to high-fidelity mock-ups in a different way than you respond to low-fidelity mock-ups. When you show people, especially nondesigners, a high-fidelity mock-up, you tend to get feedback on the details. The fonts, colors, and content. But when you show people a paper-and-pencil sketch, there *are no details* to comment on. Instead, people read these drawings as concept drawings, and they respond to that.

So, for designers, it's important not to get seduced by how easy it is to just whip out Figma, grab the components in your design system, and produce a credible mock-up. Don't do it. Start with your fat markers.

For design systems teams, though, there's an opportunity to help users choose the right tool for the job. When we wrote the first edition of this book, designers had an array of digital wireframing tools that were optimized for making sketch-fidelity drawings. We're just starting to see design systems teams consider adding sketch-fidelity elements into their toolkits. This is a fascinating trend and one we'll be following to see where it develops.

Now, let's take a look at how one large organization uses design systems...

Case study: GE design system

In 2012, GE opened GE Software in San Ramon, California. This new "Center of Excellence" (CoE) was designed to help GE improve its software game. A few years earlier, a strategic review helped the company to see just how central software had become to their business: measured in lines of code, GE was something like the 17th largest software company in the world. And yet they felt they were not treating software development with the focus it deserved.

San Ramon included a new team at GE: the GE Software User Experience Team. This small team at the heart of a giant company created their first design system in 2013 in order to scale the impact they could have. Indeed, with fewer than 50 designers to collaborate with more than 14,000 developers (inside an organization of more than 300,000 people), there was no way that this startup design team could grow quickly enough to have a meaningful effect at GE.

The team's first design system, called IIDS, for the Industrial Internet Design System, was designed by a group of internal designers with the help of a small team from Frog Design, one of the leading design firms in the world. The team built the system on top of Bootstrap, the HTML/CSS framework created by Twitter. It proved incredibly successful. Within a few years, it had been downloaded by internal developers more than 11,000 times and had been used to create hundreds of applications. It helped software teams across the company produce better looking, more consistent applications. And, perhaps just as important, it created a huge amount of visibility for the software team and the UX team at San Ramon.

With that success came some problems. To be sure, simply having a good UI kit doesn't mean that a team can produce a well-designed product. Design systems don't solve every design problem. And Bootstrap was showing its limits as a platform choice. It had helped the team achieve their first objectives: get something out quickly, provide broad coverage of UI elements, and create wide adoption by being easier to use than "roll-your-own" solutions. But Bootstrap was hard to maintain and update and was just too big for most needs.

In 2015, GE Software, having had great success as an internal service bureau, morphed into GE Digital, a revenue-generating business in its own right. Their first product was called Predix (Figure 14-3), a platform on top of which developers inside and outside of GE can build software for industrial applications. And with this change of strategy, the team realized they needed to rethink their design system. Whereas earlier the goal had been to provide broad coverage and broad adoption, the new design system would be driven by new needs: it needed to enable great Predix applications, which was a more focused problem than before. It needed to *limit* the number of UI choices rather than supporting every possible UI widget. It still needed to be easy to adopt and use—it was now intended for use by GE customers—but now it was imperative that it be easy to maintain as well.

The design system team had by this time grown to about 15 people and included design technologists (frontend developers who are passionate about both design and code), interaction designers, graphic designers, a technical writer, and a product owner.

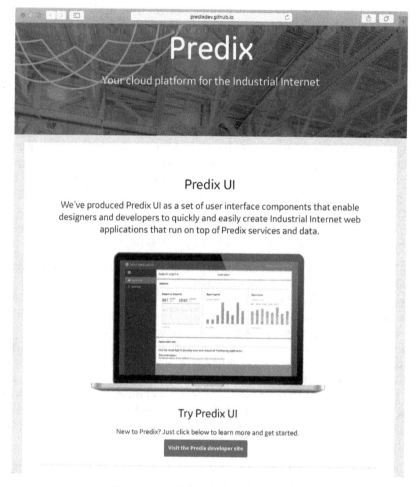

Figure 14-3. *The GE Predix design system*

The team chose to move the design system to a new technology platform (Figure 14-4). No longer based on Bootstrap, the system has instead been created with Polymer, a JavaScript framework that allows the team to implement Web Components. Web Components has emerged in the last few years as a way to enable more mature frontend development practices.

To create the new design system, the team spent nearly six months prototyping. Significantly, the team did not work in isolation. Instead, they paired with one of the application teams and thus were designing components to meet the needs of their users—in this case, the designers and developers working on the application teams. This point is really important. Collaborative design takes many forms. Sometimes it means designing with your cross-functional team. Sometimes it means designing with your end users. In this instance, it was a hybrid: designing with a cross-functional team of designers and developers *who actually are* your users.

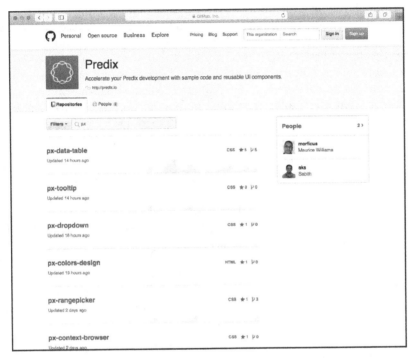

Figure 14-4. *The GE Predix design system on GitHub*

Collaborating with Geographically Distributed Teams

Physical distance is one of the biggest challenges to strong collaboration. Some of the methods we've discussed in this book become more difficult when a team isn't all in the same location. That said—as we all learned in 2020, thanks to the COVID-19 crisis—you can still find ways to collaborate when you and your team are separated by distance. Tools such as Zoom, Skype, Google Meet, and Slack can provide teams with the means to collaborate in real time. Google Docs and similar systems allow people to collaborate on documents at the same time. Team collaboration tools like Mural and Miro serve as a space for creative collaboration. Trello and wikis make it possible for teams to track information together. Design tools like Figma are built from the ground up with collaboration in mind. And a phone with a camera can make it easy to quickly share photos in an ad hoc way. All these tools can make cross-time-zone collaboration more effective and can help teams to feel virtually connected for long periods of time during the day.

Collaborating with Distributed Teams

When we talk about distributed teams, we're actually talking about a variety of different scenarios. Sometimes we mean that we're in an office in NYC with part of our team, and we need to work with other teammates who are working in the London office. Other times it means that we are on 2020-style lockdown, working from home with our pets and our kids and our partners in the same room. Sometimes we're talking about a hybrid situation—most of us are in the office, but a few folks are calling in to a meeting. What works in one of these contexts might not work in others, but there are some important ideas that you can use to make collaboration easier in any context.

Level the playing field. Have you ever called in to a meeting where you were the only person on the phone, and everyone else was sitting around the table? It's tough. Now imagine a room full of people working on sticky notes or drawing on the whiteboard, while you're sitting in your kitchen listening on the phone. It's going to be difficult—perhaps impossible—for you to make a meaningful contribution. One fix for this is to insist that your meeting-room tools be chosen so that everyone can participate. Instead of using the conference-room whiteboard, your team can open a shared document or use an online whiteboard tool like Mural or Miro. This means that everyone in the conference room will need their own laptop or tablet, but it will also ensure that everyone can collaborate as peers.

Create social connections. It can be tempting to treat online meetings in a very regimented way. Gather the team, hit the agenda hard, end on time, boom. Remote meetings start and end more abruptly than physical meetings. Think about it—when we meet in a conference room, we chat for a few minutes in the hallway before the meeting. We gossip as we take our chairs. We walk out of the room together and get a coffee together to debrief. These moments may seem incidental to the work that we do, but they are actually a crucial component of work—they give us time to build the social bonds that allow work to happen. Make the effort to create social connections across remote collaborations. Build in extra time for slow openings to your meetings. Schedule team social calls across the distance. Create social/nonwork channels in your team Slack workspaces. If you can travel to see your remote teammates, make sure to build team social events into your travel agendas.

Making Collaboration Work

Not every team will find that collaboration comes easily. Most of us begin our careers by developing our individual technical skills as designers, developers, and so on. And in many organizations, collaboration across disciplines is rare. (It's rarely taught in school as well, either as an explicit topic or in the way our educational systems are set up.) So it's no wonder that it can feel challenging.

One of the most powerful tools for improving collaboration is the Agile technique of the *retrospective* and the related practice of creating *team working agreements*. Retrospectives are regularly scheduled meetings, usually held at the end of every sprint, in which the team takes an honest look back at the past sprint. They examine what went well, what went poorly, and what the team wants to improve. Usually, the team will select a few things to work on for the next sprint. We can think of no more powerful tool for improving collaboration than the regular practice of effective retrospectives.

A team working agreement is a document that serves as a partner to the retrospective. It keeps track of how the team has chosen to work together. It's a self-created, continuously updated rule book that the team agrees to follow. At each retrospective, the team should check in with their working agreement to see if they're still following it and if they need to update it to include new agreements or remove old ones that no longer make sense.

Here's an outline for what you should consider covering in your team working agreements:

Process overview
> What kind of process are we using? Agile? If so, what flavor? How long are our iterations?

Ceremonies
> What rituals will the team observe? For example, when is stand-up each day? When do we hold planning meetings and demos?

Communication/Tools
> What systems will we use to communicate and document our work? What is our project management tool? Where do we keep our assets?

Culture/Safety/Conflict resolution
> What kind of team culture do we want? What do we need as individuals to feel safe with our teammates? What will we do when (not if!) there's conflict? How will we resolve disagreements?

Working hours
> Who works where? When are folks in the office? If we're in different locations, what accommodations will we make for time-zone differences?

Requirements and design

How do we handle requirements definition, story writing, and prioritization? When is a story ready for design? When is a design ready to be broken into stories?

Development

What practices have we settled on? Do we use pair programming? What testing style will we use? What methods will we use for source control?

Work-in-progress limits

What is our backlog and icebox size? What WIP limits exist in various stages of our process?

Deployment

What is our release cadence? How do we do story acceptance?

And any additional agreements.

Psychological Safety

Collaborative design is a creative activity. To be effective, people need to feel safe. This means physical, emotional, and psychological safety. We often hear this idea expressed in superficial ways, like "there are no bad ideas in brainstorming" or "there's no such thing as a stupid question." And while those things are true, they are certainly not sufficient. Psychological safety is more than that. Author Alla Weinberg defines psychological safety as "the shared belief that no one on the team will embarrass or punish anyone else for admitting a mistake, asking a question, or offering a new idea."

Lean UX is all about the idea that design is an iterative process. You need to try, learn, and iterate. In other words, you need to make mistakes in order to make progress. You can't do this if you and your team don't feel safe.

If you find yourself or your team stuck in a rut, experiencing high degrees of conflict, or generally acting scared, take a step back and ask, Do I feel safe on this team? Do I think my team members feel safe? If you're not sure, consider taking a step back and looking at the work of writers like Weinberg and Amy Edmondson to help you and your team address these concerns.

Wrapping Up

Collaborative design (Figure 14-5) is an evolution of the UX design process. In this chapter, we discussed how opening up the design process brings the entire team deeper into the project. We showed you practical techniques you can use to create shared understanding—the fundamental currency of Lean UX. Using tools like design systems, style guides, collaborative design sessions, Design Studio, and simple conversation, your team can build a shared understanding that allows them to move forward at a much faster pace than in traditional environments.

Figure 14-5. *A team using collaborative design techniques*

CHAPTER 15

Feedback and Research

Research is formalized curiosity. It is poking and prying with a purpose.
Zora Neale Hurston

Research with users is at the heart of UX design. Too often, though, teams out-source research work to specialized research teams. And too often, research activities take place on rare occasions—either at the beginning of a project or at the end. Lean UX solves these problems by making research both *continuous* and *collaborative*. Let's dig in to see how to do that.

In this chapter, we cover the following:

- Collaborative research techniques that you can use to build shared understanding with your team
- Continuous research techniques to build small, informal, qualitative research studies into every iteration
- How to use small units of regular research to build longitudinal research studies
- How to reconcile contradictory feedback from multiple sources
- What artifacts to test and what results you can expect from each of these tests
- How to incorporate the voice of the customer throughout the Lean UX cycle

Continuous and Collaborative Research

Lean UX takes basic UX research techniques and overlays two important ideas. First, Lean UX research is continuous. This means you build research activities into every sprint. Instead of being a costly and disruptive "big bang" process, we make it bite-sized so that we can fit it into our ongoing process. Second, Lean UX research is collaborative. This means that you don't rely on the work of specialized researchers to deliver learning to your team. Instead, research activities and responsibilities are distributed and shared across the entire team. By eliminating the handoff between researchers and team members, we increase the quality of our learning. Our goal in all of this is to create a rich *shared understanding* across the team.

Collaborative Discovery

Collaborative discovery is the process of working together as a team to test ideas in the market. It is one of the two main cross-functional techniques that create shared understanding on a Lean UX team. (Collaborative design, covered in Chapter 14, is the other.) Collaborative discovery is an approach to research that gets the entire team out of the building—literally and figuratively—to meet with and learn from customers and users. It gives everyone on the team a chance to see how the hypotheses are tested and, most important, multiplies the number of perspectives the team can use to gather customer insight.

It's essential that you and your team conduct research together; that's why we call it *collaborative discovery*. Outsourcing research dramatically reduces its value: it wastes time, it limits team building, and it filters the information through deliverables, handoffs, and interpretation. Don't do it.

Researchers sometimes feel uneasy about this approach. As trained professionals, they are right to point out that they have special knowledge that is important to the research process. We agree. That's why you should include a researcher on your team if you can. Just don't outsource the work to that person. Instead, use the researcher as an expert guide to help your team plan their work and to lead the team through their research activities. In the same way that Lean UX encourages designers to take a more facilitative approach, Lean UX asks the same of researchers. Researchers should use their expertise to help the team plan good research, ask good questions, and select the right methods for the job. Just don't do all the research for them.

Collaborative discovery in the field

Collaborative discovery is simply a way to get out into the field with your team. Here's how you do it:

1. As a team, review your questions, assumptions, hypotheses, and MVPs. Decide as a team what you need to learn. (Box 7 on the Lean UX Canvas.)

2. Working as a team, decide on your research method. (Box 8 on the Lean UX Canvas.) If you are planning to work directly with customers and users, decide who you'll need to speak to and observe to address your learning goals.

3. Create an interview guide (see the sidebar "The Interview Guide") that you can all use to guide your conversations.

4. Break your team into research pairs, mixing up the various roles and disciplines within each pair (i.e., try not to have designers paired with designers). If you are doing this research over a number of days, try to mix up the interview pairs each day so that people have a chance to share experiences with various team members.

5. Arm each pair with a version of your MVP, prototype, or other materials you want to show to the research participants.

6. Send each team out to meet with customers/users.

7. One team member interviews while the other takes notes.

8. Begin with questions, conversations, and observations.

9. Demonstrate the MVP later in the session and allow the customer to interact with it.

10. Collect notes as the customer provides feedback.

11. When the lead interviewer is done, switch roles to give the notetaker a chance to ask follow-up questions.

12. At the end of the interview, ask the customer for referrals to other people who might also provide useful feedback.

The Interview Guide

To prepare for fieldwork, create a small cheat sheet that will fit into your notebook. On your cheat sheet, write the questions and topics that you've decided to cover. This way you'll always be prepared to move the interview along.

When planning your questions, think about a sequential funnel:

- First, try to identify if the customer is in your target audience.
- Then, try to confirm any problem hypotheses you have for this segment.

Finally, if you have a prototype or mock-up with you, show this last to avoid limiting the conversation to your vision of the solution.

A collaborative discovery example

A team we worked with at PayPal set out with a clickable prototype to conduct a collaborative discovery session. The team was made up of two designers, a UX researcher, four developers, and a product manager; they split into teams of two and three. They paired each developer with a nondeveloper. Before setting out, they brainstormed what they'd like to learn from their prototype and used these ideas to write brief interview guides. Their product was targeted at a broad consumer market, so they decided to just head out to the local shopping malls scattered around their office. Each pair targeted a different mall. They spent two hours in the field, stopping strangers, asking them questions, and demonstrating their prototypes. To build up their individual skill sets, they changed roles (from lead to notetaker) an hour into their research.

When they reconvened, each pair read their notes to the rest of the team. Almost immediately they began to see patterns emerge, confirming some of their assumptions and rejecting others. Using this new information, they adjusted the design of their prototype and headed out again later that afternoon. After a full day of field research, it was clear which parts of their idea worked well and which parts would need adjusting. When they began the next sprint the following day, every member of the team was working from the same baseline of clarity, having built a shared understanding by means of collaborative discovery the day before.

Continuous Learning

Designers and researchers face a lot of pressure to force their work into a sprint framework. The problem is that some work just takes a long time, especially some kinds of research. This long-cycle work has the potential to create conflict on Agile teams. Researchers are used to planning multiweek research projects, for example. And when they try to do this on an Agile team and put their eight-week research project into the backlog, they end up having to explain at the end of every sprint why their work isn't "done." It makes everyone unhappy.

Going back to principles

When faced with a conflict like this, it's helpful to go back to principles. Remember this principle from Chapter 2? *Don't do the same thing faster.* And this one? *Beware of phases.* These principles tell us that we shouldn't try to fit an eight-week research study into a two-week sprint. Instead, we should rethink the way we plan our research and the way we think about "done" for research work.

To do that, let's consider why the Scrum framework is so insistent on the notion of *done*. Scrum says that any work you do during a sprint should be done by the end of that sprint. This is a powerful forcing function: it forces everyone to show their work. And it makes the assumption that finished work is valuable. (That's not always true, but that's the goal.)

For us then, the goal of *done* is really: "Be transparent and deliver value every sprint."

How can we use that idea when we're planning research? Well, instead of thinking about completing our eight-week study in two weeks, we can ask, "How can we be transparent and deliver value every two weeks, even as we're working on an eight-week study?" We might deliver an experience report at sprint demo meetings. We might present some early conclusions after completing half of our interviews. We might present and discuss the new questions that have come up as we've started to learn new things. Those things are all valuable to the team. They make the work transparent. They maintain the spirit of Agile while also keeping the integrity of the research work high.

Continuous research: Research is never done

A high-functioning Agile team should be doing research continuously. A critical best practice in Lean UX is building a regular cadence of customer involvement. Regularly scheduled conversations with customers let you minimize the time between hypothesis creation, experiment design, and user feedback—giving you the opportunity to validate your hypotheses quickly.

In other words, research should inform the decisions the product team is making. Since you're making decisions constantly, you want to make sure you have the latest research data at hand at all times. (And conversely, the research agenda should sometimes drive development priorities because sometimes you need to make stuff specifically support the needs of your researchers. It's a two-way conversation.)

In general, knowing you're never more than a few days away from getting customer feedback has a powerful effect on teams. It takes the pressure off of your decision making because you know that you will soon have an opportunity to get meaningful data from the market—and course correct quickly if needed.

So stop thinking in terms of research studies and research phases, and instead think of research as a continuous part of your team's operating rhythm. Share your work. Deliver value each week. Be honest about what you do and don't know. Help your team learn. The rest of this chapter will show you how.

Continuous learning in the lab: Three users every Thursday

Although you can create a standing schedule of fieldwork based on the aforementioned ideas, it's much easier (especially for companies that work with consumers) to bring customers into the building—you just need to be a little creative to get the entire team involved.

We like to use a weekly rhythm to schedule research, as demonstrated in Figure 15-1. We call this "Three, twelve, one" because it's based on the following guidelines: three users; by twelve noon; once a week.

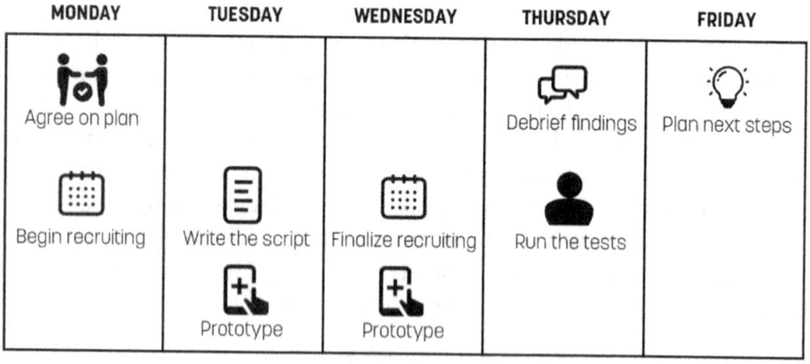

Figure 15-1. The three, twelve, one activity calendar

Here's how the team's activities break down:

Monday: Recruiting and planning
> Decide, as a team, what will be tested this week. Decide who you need to recruit for tests and start the recruiting process. Outsource this job if at all possible: it's very time-consuming (see the sidebar "A Word About Recruiting Participants" on page 144).

Tuesday: Refine the components of the test

Based on what stage your MVP is in, begin refining the design, the prototype, or the product to a point that will allow you to tell at least one complete story when your customers see it.

Wednesday: Continue refining, write the script, and finalize recruiting

Put the final touches on your MVP. Write the test script that your moderator will follow with each participant. (Your moderator should be someone on the team if at all possible.) Finalize the recruiting and schedule for Thursday's tests.

Thursday: Test!

Spend the morning testing your MVP with customers. Spend no more than an hour with each customer. Everyone on the team should take notes. The team should plan to watch from a separate location. Review the findings with the entire project team immediately after the last participant is done.

Friday: Plan

Use your new insight to decide whether your hypotheses were validated and what you need to do next.

Simplify your test environment

Many firms have established usability labs in-house—and it used to be you needed one. These days, you don't need a lab—all you need is a quiet place in your office and a computer with a network connection and a webcam. It used to be necessary to use specialized usability testing products to record sessions and connect remote observers. These days, you don't even need that. We routinely run tests with remote observers using nothing more exotic than Zoom.

The ability to connect remote observers is a key element. It makes it possible for you to bring the test sessions to team members and stakeholders who can't be present. This has an enormous impact on collaboration because it spreads understanding of your customers deep into your organization. It's hard to overstate how powerful this is.

Who should watch?

The short answer is your entire team. Like almost every other aspect of Lean UX, usability testing should be a group activity. With the entire team watching the tests, absorbing the feedback, and reacting in real time, you'll find the need for subsequent debriefings reduced. The team will learn firsthand where their efforts are succeeding and failing. Nothing is more humbling (and motivating) than seeing a user struggle with the software you just built.

> ## A Word About Recruiting Participants
>
> Recruiting, scheduling, and confirming participants is time intensive. Save your team from this additional overhead by offloading the work to a dedicated recruiter. Some companies have hired internal recruiters to do this work as part of their DesignOps or ResearchOps team, while others outsource the work to a third party. In either case, the cost is worth it. The recruiter does the work and gets paid for each participant they bring in. In addition, your recruiter takes care of the screening, scheduling, and replacement of no-shows on testing day. Third-party recruiters typically charge for each participant they recruit. You'll also have to budget for whatever compensation you offer to the participants themselves.

Continuous research: Some examples

Companies operationalize continuous research in many different ways. For example, the team at ABN AMRO, a bank in the Netherlands, runs what they call a Customer Validation Carousel once a week. This weekly user research event is structured like speed dating. Each week, five customers come into the company's offices. Each customer is set up at their own research station. Then a group of interviewers come into the room and spread out, each sitting with one customer. (At ABN AMRO, many of the interviewers are "people who do research"—in other words, designers and product people rather than trained researchers. Because of this, the trained researchers on staff work with them before the event to help them create their research plan and discussion guides. Interviews are often conducted by a pair of interviewers who work together and take turns interviewing and taking notes.)

The interviewers conduct 15-minute interviews with each participant. When the 15 minutes are up, each interviewer or pair gets up and moves to the next participant—kind of like musical chairs. In this way, each interviewer gets to speak to each participant. After everyone has spoken with everyone else, the customers leave and the interviewers convene to debrief. Normally, each interviewer is assigned to a single topic, but even though they may not be working on the same set of questions, the debrief is valuable, helping them better understand the customers and helping them to interpret the data that they've just collected. They capture learnings from this event on a single-page insight template and then add these documents to the company's shared insights database. Researcher Ike Breed, who helped set up this process, told us that this sharing step really democratized research. "People thought the insights database was a really formal thing. They asked, 'you mean I can put something in there?'" By opening the process up to contribution from a wider group, it helped the product and design teams feel more ownership of the customer insights process and the data that was collected as part of that process.

Testing Tuesdays

Another researcher we spoke to told us about how he started a practice called "Testing Tuesdays" at his company, a financial services firm building consumer-facing technology. Andrew Bourne was hired there as a usability researcher. When he arrived, he discovered a long backlog of work waiting for him. As he worked through the backlog, he started reporting on the research results at every Sprint Demo, which, at his company, took place every Tuesday. Because he had such a large backlog of work, there was always something new to report. To help make sure that his reports got heard by everyone who was interested, he started publicizing the contents of his briefing in advance using email announcements. He'd announce, "This week, I'll be reporting on X." This had two really positive effects. First, it got people to show up for his briefings—often many more people were interested in the results than he'd anticipated. Additionally, product people started coming to him asking for his partnership in the research that *they* wanted to do. In other words, it grew the demand for research. And not just usability studies. The folks coming to him were asking for all kinds of research—including early-stage formative studies.

Continuous Research at Sperientia Labs

Sperientia Labs is a user experience research agency of about 30 people based in Puebla, Mexico. Sperientia delivers research to clients in a unique format: they use a series of one-week research sprints. "We use an approach in which the Agile framework is always in mind," says founder Victor M. González.

This approach has several benefits. First, González says that most of their clients are already working in an Agile rhythm. This allows Sperientia to synchronize their timeline with the timeline of the clients.

Another benefit is the rapid way that these cycles deliver results. Sperientia delivers discovery interviews and usability tests over the course of a highly structured week. They plan and recruit on Friday, continue recruiting and prepping on Monday, then run tests with between three and six participants on Tuesday and Wednesday morning. By Wednesday afternoon, they hold a debrief session with their clients. "In many cases, this debrief is all the clients need, and they can get to work immediately on what they've learned," González says. Still, Sperientia uses Thursdays to capture the results and recommendations in a report, and then meets with the clients on Friday morning to review the findings in detail. After lunch on Friday, they're ready to begin planning their next cycle.

Now, not all research objectives can be met in a week, and a typical Sperientia research program is 3 to 12 months long. So even though they use one-week research cycles throughout all of their programs, they are not limited to answering only questions that can be answered in a single week. Instead, they use continuous one-week cycles to address a much broader range of questions.

The agency works with a variety of client research objectives: they help clients understand and develop value propositions, understand users' jobs to be done, and evaluate the usability and design of their offerings.

By using a program of multiple one-week cycles, Sperientia can run research programs that grow and evolve as they learn. They can run research programs that keep pace with the development of a product. They can run programs that are longitudinal in nature. And though their approach is fundamentally qualitative (based on one-on-one sessions with users and customers), they can build programs that gather quantitative data by asking the same questions week over week.

Recently, Sperientia began experimenting with a new two-week research sprint format. They use this format when they have to answer questions that involve some kind of prototype. In these cases, they will extend the cycle to include a week of prototype development, followed by their typical research week. To accomplish this, they augment the research team to include designers who can help them create prototypes for testing.

So working with these short one-week cycles helps the agency match their client's pace, helps them deliver rapid and continuous results, and has one bonus benefit. González describes it this way: "We get to have our weekends with the peace of mind that we are done!"

Making Sense of the Research: A Team Activity

Whether your team does fieldwork or labwork, research generates a lot of raw data. Making sense of this can be time-consuming and frustrating—so the process is often handed over to specialists who are asked to synthesize research findings. You shouldn't do this. Instead, work as hard as you can to make sense of the data as a team.

As soon as possible after the research sessions are over—preferably the same day, if not then the following day—gather the team together for a review session. When the team has reassembled, ask everyone to read their findings to one another. One really efficient way to do this is to transcribe the notes people read out loud onto index cards or sticky notes and then sort the notes into themes. This process of reading, grouping, and discussing gets everyone's input out on the table and builds the shared understanding that you seek. With themes identified, you and your team can then determine the next steps for your MVP.

Confusion, contradiction, and (lack of) clarity

As you and your team collect feedback from various sources and try to synthesize your findings, you will inevitably come across situations in which your data presents you with contradictions. How do you make sense of it all? Here are a couple of ways to maintain your momentum and ensure that you're maximizing your learning.

Look for patterns

As you review the research, keep an eye out for patterns in the data. These patterns reveal multiple instances of user opinion that represent elements to explore. If something doesn't fall into a pattern, it is likely an outlier.

Place your outliers in a "parking lot"

Tempting as it is to ignore outliers (or try to serve them in your solution), don't do it. Instead, create a parking lot or backlog. As your research progresses over time (remember: you're doing this every week), you might discover other outliers that match the pattern. Be patient.

Verify with other sources

If you're not convinced the feedback you're seeing through one channel is valid, look for it in other channels. Are the customer support emails reflecting the same concerns as your usability studies? Is the value of your prototype echoed with customers inside and outside your office? If not, your sample might have been disproportionately skewed.

Identifying Patterns over Time

Typical UX research programs are structured to get a conclusive answer: you will plan to do enough research to conclusively answer a question or set of questions. Lean UX research takes a different approach. It puts a priority on being continuous—which means that you are structuring your research activities very differently. Instead of running big studies, you are seeing a small number of users every week. This means that some questions might remain open over a couple of weeks. One big benefit, though, is that interesting patterns can reveal themselves over time.

For example, over the course of regular test sessions from 2008 to 2011, the team at TheLadders watched an interesting change in their customers' attitudes over time. In 2008, when they first began meeting with job seekers on a regular basis, they would discuss various ways to communicate with employers. One of the options they proposed was SMS. In 2008, the audience, made up of high-income earners in their late 40s and early 50s, showed a strong disdain for SMS as a legitimate communication method. To them, it was something their kids did (and that perhaps they did with their kids), but it was certainly not a "proper" way to conduct a job search.

By 2011, though, SMS messages had taken off in the United States. As text messaging gained acceptance in business culture, audience attitudes began to soften. Week after week, as they sat with job seekers, they began to see opinions about SMS change. The team saw job seekers become far more likely to use SMS in a midcareer job search than they would have just a few years earlier.

The team at TheLadders would never have recognized this as an audience-wide trend were it not for two things. First, they were speaking with a sample of their audience, week in and week out. Additionally, though, the team took a systematic approach to investigating long-term trends. As part of their regular interaction with customers, they always asked a regular set of level-setting questions to capture the "vital signs" of the job seeker's search—no matter what other questions, features, or products they were testing. By doing this, the team was able to establish a baseline and address bigger trends over time. The findings about SMS would not have changed the team's understanding of their audience if they'd represented just a few anecdotal data points. But aggregated over time, these data points became part of a very powerful dataset.

When planning your research, it's important to consider not just the urgent questions—the things you want to learn over the next few weeks. You should also consider the big questions. You still need to plan big standalone studies to get at some of these questions. But with some planning, you should be able to work a lot of long-term learning into your weekly studies.

Test what you've got

To maintain a regular cadence of user testing, your team must adopt a "test-what-you-got" policy. Whatever is ready on testing day is what goes in front of the users. This policy liberates your team from rushing toward testing day deadlines—or, worse, delaying research activities in pursuit of some elusive "perfect" moment. Instead, when you adopt a "test-what-you-got" approach, you'll find yourself taking advantage of your weekly test sessions to get insight on whatever is ready, and this will create insight for you at every stage of design and development. You must, however, set expectations properly for the type of feedback you'll be able to generate with each type of artifact.

Sketches. Feedback collected on sketches helps you validate the value of your concept (see Figure 15-2). They're great conversation prompts to support interviews, and they help to make abstract concepts concrete, which helps generate shared understanding. What you won't get from sketches is detailed, step-by-step feedback on the process, insight about specific design elements, or even meaningful feedback on copy choices. You *won't* be able to learn much (if anything) about the usability of your concept.

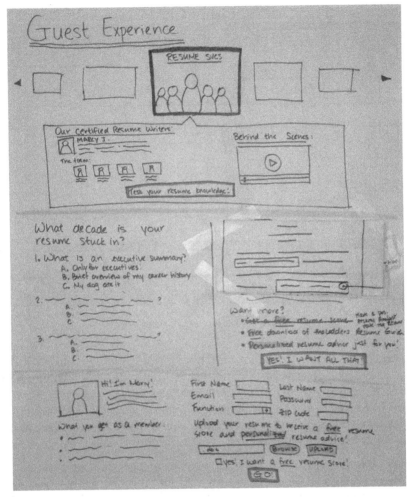

Figure 15-2. *Example of a sketch that can be used with customers*

Static wireframes. Showing test participants wireframes (Figure 15-3) lets you assess the information hierarchy and layout of your experience. In addition, you'll get feedback on taxonomy, navigation, and information architecture.

You'll receive the first trickles of workflow feedback, but at this point your test participants are focused primarily on the words on the page and the selections they're making. Wireframes provide a good opportunity to begin testing copy choices.

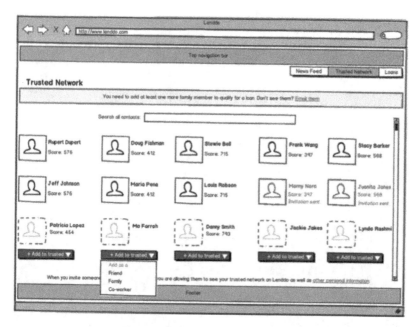

Figure 15-3. *Example of a wireframe*

High-fidelity visual mock-ups (not clickable).   Moving into high-fidelity visual-design assets, you receive much more detailed feedback. Test participants will be able to respond to branding, aesthetics, and visual hierarchy, as well as aspects of figure/ground relationships, grouping of elements, and the clarity of your calls to action. Your test participants will also (almost certainly) weigh in on the effectiveness of your color palette. (See Figure 15-4.)

Nonclickable mock-ups still don't let your customers interact naturally with the design or experience the workflow of your solution. Instead of watching your users click, tap, and swipe, you need to ask them what they would expect and then validate those responses against your planned experience.

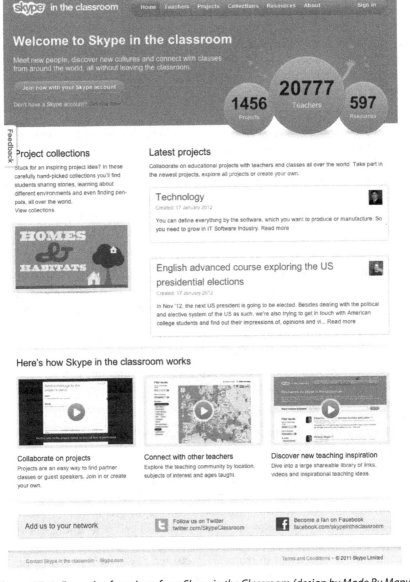

Figure 15-4. *Example of mock-up from Skype in the Classroom (design by Made By Many)*

Clickable mock-ups. Clickable mock-ups, like that shown in Figure 15-4, increase the fidelity of the interaction by linking together a set of static assets into a simulation of the product experience. These days, most design tools make it easy to link together a number of static screens to produce these types of mock-ups. Visually, they can be high, medium, or even low fidelity. The value here is not so much the visual polish but rather the ability to simulate workflow and to observe how users interact with your designs.

Designers used to have limited tool choices for creating clickable mock-ups, but in recent years, we've seen a huge proliferation of tools. Some tools are optimized for making mobile mock-ups, others are for the web, and still others are platform neutral. Most have no ability to work with data, but with some (like Axure), you can create basic data-driven or conditional logic-driven simulations. Additionally, design tools such as Figma, Sketch, InVision, and Adobe XD include "mirror" features with which you can see your design work in real time on mobile devices and link screens together to create prototypes without special prototyping tools.

Coded prototypes. Coded prototypes are useful because they have the best ability to deliver high fidelity in terms of *functionality*. This makes for the closest-to-real simulation that you can put in front of your users. It replicates the design, behavior, and workflow of your product. You can test with real data. You can integrate with other systems. All of this makes coded prototypes very powerful; it also makes them the most complex to produce. But because the feedback you gain is based on such a close simulation, you can treat that feedback as more authoritative than the feedback you gain from other simulations.

Monitoring Techniques for Continuous and Collaborative Discovery

In the preceding discussions, we looked at ways to use qualitative research on a regular basis to evaluate your hypotheses. However, as soon as you launch your product or feature, your customers will begin giving you constant feedback—and not only on your product. They will tell you about themselves, about the market, about the competition. This insight is invaluable—and it comes into your organization from every corner. Seek out these treasure troves of customer intelligence within your organization and harness them to drive your ongoing product design and research, as depicted in Figure 15-5.

Figure 15-5. *Customers can provide feedback through many channels*

Customer service

Customer support agents talk to more customers on a daily basis than you will talk to over the course of an entire project. There are multiple ways to harness their knowledge:

- Reach out to them and ask them what they're hearing from customers about the sections of the product on which you're working.

- Hold regular monthly meetings with them to understand the trends. What do customers love this month? What do they hate?

- Tap into their deep product knowledge to learn how they would solve the challenges your team is working on. Include them in design sessions and design reviews.

- Incorporate your hypotheses into their call scripts. One of the cheapest ways to test your ideas is to suggest it as a fix to customers calling in with relevant complaints.

In the mid-2000s, Jeff ran the UX team at a midsized tech company in Portland, Oregon. One of the ways that team prioritized the work they did was by regularly checking the pulse of the customer base. The team did this with a standing monthly meeting with customer service representatives. Each month, Customer Service would provide the UX team with the top 10 things customers were complaining about. The UX team then used this information to focus their efforts and to subsequently measure the efficacy of their work. At the end of the month, the next conversation with Customer Service gave the team a clear indication of whether or not their efforts were bearing fruit. If the issue was not receding in the top-10 list, the solutions had not worked.

This approach generated an additional benefit. The Customer Service team realized there was someone listening to their insights and began proactively sharing customer feedback above and beyond the monthly meeting. The dialogue that was created provided the UX team with a continuous feedback loop to inform and test product hypotheses.

On-site feedback surveys

Set up a feedback mechanism in your product with which customers can send you their thoughts regularly. Here are a few options:

- Simple email forms
- Customer support forums
- Third-party community sites

You can repurpose these tools for research by doing things like the following:

- Counting how many inbound emails you're getting from a particular section of the site
- Participating in online discussions and testing some of your hypotheses
- Exploring community sites to discover and recruit hard-to-find types of users

These inbound customer feedback channels provide feedback from the point of view of your most active and engaged customers. Here are a few tactics for getting other points of view.

Search logs. Search terms are clear indicators of what customers are seeking on your site. Search patterns indicate what they're finding and what they're not finding. Repeated queries with slight variations show a user's challenge in finding certain information.

One way to use search logs for MVP validation is to launch a test page for the feature you're planning. Following the search, logs will inform you as to whether the test content (or feature) on that page is meeting the user's needs. If users continue to search on variations of that content, your experiment has failed.

Site usage analytics.   Site usage logs and analytics packages—especially funnel analyses—show how customers are using the site, where they're dropping off, and how they try to manipulate the product to do the things they need or expect it to do. Understanding these reports provides real-world context for the decisions the team needs to make.

In addition, use analytics tools to determine the success of experiments that have launched publicly. How has the experiment shifted usage of the product? Are your efforts achieving the outcome you defined? These tools provide an unbiased answer.

If you're just starting to build a product, *build usage analytics into it from day one*. Third-party metrics products like Kissmetrics and MixPanel make it easy and inexpensive to implement this functionality, and provide invaluable information to support continuous learning.

A/B testing.   A/B testing is a technique, originally developed by marketers, to gauge which of two (or more) relatively similar concepts achieve the defined goal more effectively. When applied in the Lean UX framework, A/B testing becomes a powerful tool to determine the validity of your hypotheses. Applying A/B testing is relatively straightforward after your ideas evolve into working code. Here's how it works:

- Take the proposed solution and release it to your audience. However, instead of letting every customer see it, release it only to a small subset of users.

- Measure the performance of your solution for that audience. Compare it to the other group (your control cohort) and note the differences.

- Did your new idea move the needle in the right direction? If it did, you've got a winning idea.

- If not, you've got an audience of customers that might make good targets for further research. What did they think of the new experience? Would it make sense to reach out to them for some qualitative research?

The tools for A/B testing are widely available and can be inexpensive. There are third-party commercial tools like Optimizely. There also are open source A/B testing frameworks available for every major platform. Regardless of the tools you choose, the trick is to make sure the changes you're making are small enough and the population you select is large enough that any change in behavior can be attributed with confidence to the change you've made. If you change too many things, any behavioral change cannot be directly attributed to your exact hypothesis.

Wrapping Up

In this chapter, we covered many ways to validate your hypotheses. We looked at collaborative discovery and continuous learning techniques. We discussed how to build a weekly Lean testing process and covered what you should test and what to expect from those tests. We looked at ways to monitor your customer experience in a Lean UX context, and we touched on the power of A/B testing.

These techniques, used in conjunction with the processes outlined in Chapter 4 and Chapter 5, make up the full Lean UX process loop. Your goal is to get through this loop as often as possible, refining your thinking with each iteration.

In the next section, we move away from process and take a look at how to integrate Lean UX into your organization. We'll cover the organizational shifts you'll need to make to support the Lean UX approach, whether you're a startup, large company, or a digital agency.

CHAPTER 16

Integrating Lean UX and Agile

Ask anyone at any organization what the default way of working is for them, and the answer will invariably be "We're doing Agile!" Follow that question with "And how's that working out for you?" and in most cases they'll raise their hand and shake it from side to side in the "meh, it's just OK" gesture.

Agile was born of developers, 17 of them in fact, representing emerging ways of working that had emerged from their frustration with older engineering processes and the unpredictability of software development. At a weekend gathering in Utah in 2001, these software developers put together a series of principles they called the Agile Manifesto.[1] If you haven't read it (you should, it's short), you'd be surprised to find there isn't much prescribed "process" in the Agile Manifesto. There's nothing in there that says, "You shall stand up every day at 9:15 with your team" or "You will work in two-week cycles called sprints." Those are techniques taken from specific Agile methods, like Scrum and Extreme Programming (XP), methods that were invented by many of the folks who came together to create the Agile Manifesto itself. Instead of capturing specific practices, the authors of the Manifesto listed values and principles for highly collaborative, customer-centered software development. The most compelling line in the entire manifesto—and in our opinion the basis for true agility—is "[We value] responding to change over following a plan."

That's the heart of it, really. If you work in a way that invites learning, embrace that learning in a humble manner, and change your plan based on what you've learned, you are being agile.

---

1 "Manifesto for Agile Software Development," accessed June 18, 2021, *http://agilemanifesto.org*.

In the 20 years since the Manifesto was created, this approach to doing work has become the default way of working in most organizations (or at least, the default aspiration). These Agile ideas reached well beyond software development teams and are now being applied to everything from strategic planning and leadership to human resources, finance, marketing, and, of course, design.

The most well-known form of Agile is Scrum, a lightweight framework invented primarily by Jeff Sutherland and Ken Schwaber in the mid-1990s. (Yes, Scrum has been around longer than the Agile Manifesto.) And yet for all its popularity, Scrum itself has only recently begun to think about how design fits into the process. Until as recently as November 2020, *The Scrum Guide* (*http://www.scrumguides.org*)—the official documentation of Scrum—had never mentioned user experience or design in any way. As great design and customer-centricity become increasingly important success factors in technology products, designers and Agile practitioners alike have struggled to figure out exactly how to integrate themselves into Agile processes. While the rest of Lean UX describes an Agile way of working, this chapter will help answer some questions about how Lean UX fits into the mechanics of Agile methods, and, in particular, we'll focus on design within the context of Scrum.

Make the Agile Process Your Own

We often get asked how newly formed Agile teams should work. Should they use Scrum? Should they work in two-week sprints? What level of formality should they implement in order to be successful? With so many stories of frustration with Agile transformations, teams and leaders want to get it right as quickly as possible and minimize pain, frustration, and decreased productivity. You could spend the next 10 years reading all of the books on Scrum best practices, but when you boil it down to the core, you're left with the following components, which make a great starting point for any team:

- Work in short cycles.
- Deliver value at the end of each cycle.
- Hold a brief daily planning meeting (or Daily Scrum).
- Hold a retrospective after every cycle.

You can spend a lot of time debating all of the other components of Scrum (as well as the things people *think* are part of Scrum but are never mentioned in *The Scrum Guide*), but these four basic elements provide all you need to increase the agility of your team. A team with a dedicated lineup will work together to figure out what they can get done in each cycle. They will meet daily to determine what the next most important set of things is to do, and, critically, they will review the efficacy of their process after every cycle.

In fact, it's no exaggeration to say that retrospectives, when used properly, are the key to building a cohesive, cross-functional Agile team. Scrum doesn't tell you how to fit designers or design work into a sprint or how to handle design work in the backlog, but if your team tries one way to build design into the Scrum process, runs that for a sprint or two, and then retrospects to determine how well that worked, you've begun the process of owning your Agile process. If you remove the prescriptive ethos of Scrum from the process and instead apply the philosophical lens of the Agile Manifesto, then you are, indeed, responding to change over following a plan. In this case, the plan is the rigid prescription of Agile process; the change you are responding to is your understanding of how well that prescription worked for you and your team. If it works well, fantastic! Keep doing it. But if it failed to achieve what you hoped for, change course. Now you're *being* Agile rather than just *doing* it.

This is why retrospectives are so powerful and why they're the one Scrum event we recommend more than any other. Honest, blameless retrospectives give a team a regular opportunity to adjust how they work. A retrospective looks back at the last cycle or two and asks, *What has been working well? What hasn't been working so well? What are we going to change moving forward?* The best part of approaching a process this way is that the risk of changing your process is minimal. The longest you'll have to live with a change is the length of your sprint. While this chapter will give you many ways to build an integrated Lean UX and Scrum process, whatever you do, make sure that you use retrospectives to examine what you do. If the techniques that we recommend don't work for your team, change them, mix and match them, or throw them out. Your version of Agile (or Scrum) will be different than any other team's. This is OK. In fact, we'd argue that's the whole point of being agile.

Redefining "Done"

When is software done? We wrote about this in Chapter 3. When you're working to create an outcome, you need to ship software (the output) and then see if it creates the outcome you want. You can't ship software until you're "done." But you're not really *finished* until you've "validated" that software.

In Scrum, nothing can go live to a user until it is "done." This makes perfect sense. You need to make sure that the software you're releasing meets certain shared quality standards (what Scrum calls "the definition of done") and that it delivers the functionality that you and your team have planned (what Scrum calls the "acceptance criteria"). The definition of done is created by the team, and the acceptance criteria are usually set by the product manager or product owner. Together, these standards ensure that each piece of work is complete, works as designed, and is bug-free and stable enough to go to production. For most Scrum teams, though, this is the end of their involvement with that piece of software. This end point, though, completely fails to take responsibility for outcomes and reflects a much older idea of the nature of software.

When we started our careers, software came in a box. If that sounds weird to you, it might be even weirder to know that when Jeff was a kid, his dad would bring home the punch cards on which software came in the 1970s. In both of those cases, more than 20 years apart, software was static. It had an end state. We could package it in boxes or on paper cards. Fast-forward another 20 years, and these concepts seem ridiculous now. Software doesn't come in a box and is no longer static. Today we build systems that are updated continually and can be optimized indefinitely. It's easy, today, to argue that software is *never* done. This makes the question "When are we done?" a difficult one to answer. But we need to answer it because it helps answer other, even more important questions. Do we move on to the next feature or not? Does the team get rewarded or chastised? Does the stakeholder get their bonus?

Scrum, with its concepts of "acceptance criteria" and "definition of done," has given teams a clear set of targets to hit. But those targets only go so far. As we've said, they ensure that the software "works as designed." But "works as designed" only tells us that the software consistently does what we told it to do. Unfortunately, that's not enough. We also need to know if the software created value. *Did anyone find the feature we just shipped? Did they try it? Were they successful using it? Did they come back and use it again? Did they pay us for it?* In other words, we need to know if it created an outcome.

So how do our teams know when the work is finished? When do they know when to move on to the next initiative? We need to add a concept here: the concept of "validated." And getting to validated starts with our customers.

We validate our work after it's "done." After it's "accepted." After it's in the hands of our customers. We do this by measuring their behavior. We do this by listening to their needs and assessing if our features meet those needs, and then iterating until we meet those needs. Over and over again. It turns out designers are very good at doing this work.

By expanding our idea of done from "works as designed" to "validated with customers," we shift what Scrum teams are working toward. Instead of focusing on shipping features, they are focused on making customers successful. Design is an integral part of this, because design provides many of the tools needed to understand customers and refine solutions to better meet their needs. If a feature's definition of done is reframed as an outcome, the team has no choice but to test early versions of their idea, interact with customers to understand how things can be improved, and design optimized versions of the feature to meet those ever-changing needs.

Here's an example. Traditionally expressed acceptance criteria for a password authentication flow:

- Requires password entry
- Password meets basic requirement guidelines
- Password is entered correctly and user is verified into the system
- Password recovery link is active
- Error message displays when password is entered incorrectly
- After three failed attempts, access is blocked

Reframed criteria for the same feature:

- Percentage of users successfully authenticating on first try is 99% or higher
- Number of password recovery attempts is reduced by 90%
- Percentage of calls to the call center asking for password reset reduced by 75%

In the traditional example, the team builds and releases a set of features that work as designed. With the second definition, the team is not done until the customer is demonstrably more successful than they are today. This method reflects the modern nature of software and requires the intervention and inclusion of research, discovery, and design in the Scrum process. This recalibration of the team's goal does not negate the value of traditional acceptance criteria. We still want to ship stable, high-quality, high-performance, secure code to production. However, that's not enough. Those attributes are table stakes. None of that matters if it doesn't make the customer more successful.

We're Still Doing Staggered Sprints. Why?

In May 2007, Desiree Sy published "Adapting Usability Investigations for Agile User-Centered Design" in the *Journal of Usability Studies*.[2] Sy is one of the first people to try to combine Agile and UX, and many of us were excited by the solutions she was proposing. In the 2007 article, Sy describes in detail her idea of a productive integration of Agile and user-centered design. She called it cycle 0 (though it has come to be referred to popularly as either "sprint zero" or sometimes "staggered sprints").

---

2 Desirée Sy, "Adapting Usability Investigations for Agile User-Centered Design," *Journal of Usability Studies* 2, no. 3 (May 2007): 112–132, *https://oreil.ly/Bhxq1*.

In short, Sy, along with Lynn Miller, described a process in which design activity takes place one sprint ahead of development. Work is designed and validated during the "design sprint" and then passed off into the development stream to be implemented during the development sprint, as is illustrated in Figure 16-1.

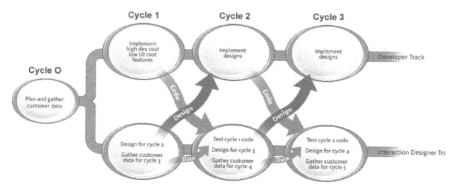

Figure 16-1. *Sy and Miller's "Staggered Sprints" model*

Many teams have misinterpreted this model, though. Sy always advocated strong collaboration between designers and developers during *both* the design *and* development sprints. Many teams have missed this critical point and instead have created workflows in which designers and developers communicate by handoff—creating a kind of mini-waterfall process.

For teams transitioning from waterfall to Agile, there's a benefit to working this way. It teaches you to work in shorter cycles and to divide your work into sequential pieces. However, this model works best as a transition. It is not where you want your team to end up.

Here's why: it becomes very easy to create a situation in which the entire team is never working on the same thing at the same time. You never realize the benefits of cross-functional collaboration because the different disciplines are focused on different things. Without that collaboration, you don't build shared understanding, so you end up relying heavily on documentation and handoffs for communication.

There's another reason this process is less than ideal: it can create unnecessary waste. You waste time creating documentation to describe what happened during the design sprints. And if developers haven't participated in the design sprint, they haven't had a chance to assess the work for feasibility or scope. That conversation doesn't happen until handoff. Can they actually build the specified designs in the next two weeks? If not, the work that went into designing those elements is wasted.

Despite these drawbacks, many teams still work in staggered sprints today. In our experience, there are several potential root causes for this:

Design team is not integrated into the "dev" process
In many companies, design is still a shared service operating as an internal agency. Designers aren't assigned to a specific Scrum team. They are seen as a dependency for the software development work to start. By having designers work a sprint ahead, the design work can "feed the machine" of software development.

Software development is outsourced
Some organizations still outsource their software development. In a world where software is the engine of business and growth, this is a staggeringly risky Achilles' heel. Nevertheless, if the coding is being done by a third-party provider, they will want to see "final" designs before they estimate and start the work. Staggered sprints make that possible for teams that work with outsourced partners.

Cargo cult Agile
Some organizations have brought in Agile processes to increase the efficiency and productivity of software development, not for the ability to change course based on new learnings and insights. In this case, the organization operates as a software factory, churning out features as fast as possible. While the work may be chunked up into sprints and Agile vocabulary used throughout the organization, the priority is still to simply ship features. These organizations typically focus on deadlines and rarely take the time to iterate and improve features through feedback and validation. Staggered sprints provide the feature factory with fodder for production. Collaboration between designers and developers is minimal, as handoffs and deliverables still form the foundation for conversation between them.

Staggered sprints are a symptom of an organization that hasn't fully embraced agility. Their use is a stepping-stone in the right direction but a clear indication that the team hasn't arrived yet. Your goal should be to build greater collaboration and transparency between designers and developers while reducing the waste of document handoffs, lengthy design reviews, and feature negotiations.

Dual-Track Agile

Dual-track Agile is a model that integrates product discovery and delivery work into one process for the same team. This is the most successful model we've seen to date for bringing Lean UX work successfully into the Agile process. In many ways, dual-track Agile is what Sy and Miller were trying to convey with their staggered-sprint model. However, for dual-track Agile to work, one team must do both kinds of work—discovery (Lean UX) and delivery.

Some teams interpret dual-track Agile as two types of work for two separate groups of people.

We don't like this model primarily because it divides the product development team into smaller (or, worse, separate) squads who then inevitably have to come back together to build a shared understanding. In practice, we've seen teams run into the following problems:

Separate discovery and delivery teams: One antipattern we've witnessed several times is teams splitting up who does the discovery and who does the delivery on their team. Often the UX designer and/or the product manager take on the bulk of the discovery work. The engineers are delegated early delivery work. This effectively recreates the mini-waterfalls of staggered sprints, as described earlier. The shared understanding breaks down, slowing the pace of decision-making and reducing the team's cohesion, productivity, and learning.

Limited knowledge of how to do discovery: Building a dual-track Agile process assumes that your team knows how to do discovery. There are many tools that you can use to build feedback loops into a discovery backlog. Without a broader knowledge of these tools, teams resort to the ones they're most familiar with and often pick suboptimal tactics for learning. If you have access to researchers, try to add them to your team. At the very least, seek out their input as new discovery initiatives begin. Seasoned practitioners can teach your team the best method for your needs and can help you plan your discovery work.

Not feeding back evidence from the delivery work to the discovery backlog: This challenge is symptomatic of an organization that is still thinking incrementally. After a feature makes it from discovery to delivery, the team will implement it as designed and ship it. The great thing about this is that, as soon as it's live, this new feature begins to provide a new set of data about how well it's working and where to focus your next discovery activities. You just have to pay attention—and get the team to pay attention. Make sure that your team is continuing to collect feedback on shipped features and using that information to regularly assess the prioritization of their discovery work.

Dual-track works when it's one team

The best way to think of dual-track is that it's two types of work—product discovery and product delivery—performed by *one team* (Figure 16-2). Discovery work consists of active learning through design and research activities, as well as passive learning through inbound analytics of features and products already in the market. In order to build shared understanding, we strive to have as many team members participate in each activity as possible. The quantity of discovery and delivery work will fluctuate from sprint to sprint. This is normal, and you can anticipate this as you make plans.

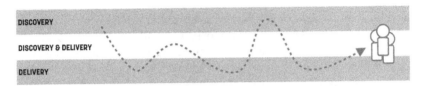

Figure 16-2. *Dual-rack Agile works when it's one team.*
Image concept: Gary Pedretti and Pawel Mysliwiec

If you're doing discovery work right, you're changing and potentially killing a lot of ideas. We don't do discovery work simply to validate every feature we have in our backlog. Instead, we're testing and learning, and sometimes that means we kill features before we ship them. Again, this is *being agile* and it's exactly the reason Agile was conceived in the first place. Without discovery work, Agile ends up just being the engine of the software factory.

Planning dual-track work

Over years of practice, we've tried many different ways of accounting for both types of work in the Scrum process. We've tried to carve out a specific amount of time in each sprint for discovery work to take place, but that was unsatisfying, because in some sprints there was none to be done, while in others it was the bulk of the work. We've tried Marty Cagan's approach of dividing the work between disciplines (design and PMs do the discovery, engineers do the delivery), but the overhead of handoffs, negotiations, and debates reduced the team's ability to respond to change. Overall, we've found that ensuring the entire team shifts its workload depending on the current sprint's needs is the best option. In fact, it is the most agile option. It allows the team to adjust its activities based on what it's learning, thereby ensuring that the most important work happens next. Sometimes that work is discovery, and other times it's delivery.

To make dual-track Agile successful and to bring Lean UX into the daily workflow of your Scrum team, there are some structural elements that are critical to that integration delivering the results your team seeks.

A dedicated designer on every team: There is no compromise here. Without a dedicated designer on the Scrum team, what you have is a software engineering team. While that team will absolutely deliver a user experience, it will not be of the same level of quality without a designer's input. What's more, that team will be lacking the skills to do good discovery work: they will focus exclusively on writing code. As we mentioned before, the production of code is no longer the goal for great digital product development—it's the means to an end. The goal is to produce meaningful changes in the behaviors of our customers. Without a deep understanding of the customer and how to best serve those needs, your product will fail. Designers bring that to the team.

Design and discovery work is a first-class citizen of the backlog: The short of it is this: one backlog. Development work, QA work, design work, research work, you name it—it all goes on one backlog, prioritized together with the same team doing all of that work. As soon as the work is divided between more than one backlog, the team will look to one of them as the "primary" one and the other(s) will go neglected. You can and should have both tracks of the work managed in the same backlog. You can certainly differentiate the different types of work in your backlog (see experiment stories, below), but it all must end up in the same project management tool, no matter whether you use a physical Scrum board or JIRA or something else.

Using one backlog and treating all work in the same way ensures the team understands that all of these components are necessary for the success of your product. It visualizes the Lean UX work in a way that puts it on the same level as software development work (which is always weighted the highest in our experience). It also highlights the trade-offs that will need to be made in order for the discovery work to take place.

Often this will bring up questions of velocity. "Won't we reduce our velocity if we do all this discovery work?" If you're only measuring the velocity of delivery, then the answer is yes. Mature dual-track teams measure both the velocity of delivery as well as the velocity of discovery (or learning). These teams realize that, as the quantity of learning work increases, it will inevitably reduce the quantity of delivery. This is because the same group of people is doing both types of work. This is also OK, because at the end of the day, we're trying to maximize how effective the team is, and we do that by tracking outcomes, not by tracking how many stories it completes or how much software it builds.

There are a couple of ways to represent Lean UX work in your backlog. (See Figure 16-3.) You can represent it as a standalone story. (*The Scrum Guide* calls stories Product Backlog Items or PBIs.) Or you can integrate the work into the story itself, ensuring that no feature gets shipped without discovery and design work taking place.

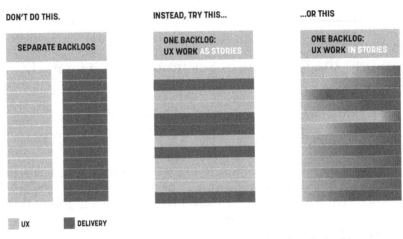

Figure 16-3. *Common patterns to manage UX work in the backlog*

Cross-functional participation in learning activities: Lean UX brings with it many types of learning activities. These activities may be led by designers or researchers or even product managers, but they should be practiced and attended by the entire team. The more the team can learn together, the less time is spent sharing and debating the learning and more time can be spent deciding what to do about the things we've learned. This latter is a far more productive conversation and use of the team's time. We're not saying that every team member needs to take part in every research activity. We do think that everyone should participate to some degree, and that participation should be a regular part of their work activity—not a special event.

Make participating in the discovery process the path of least resistance. Broadcast your customer conversations internally so others can watch from their desks. If a colleague is uncomfortable speaking with a customer, bring them along and make them the notetaker. Measure what Jared Spool refers to as "exposure hours."[3] Exposure hours is a measure of the amount of time each member of your team is *directly* exposed to users. Make sure each member of

---

3 Jared M. Spool, "Fast Path to a Great UX – Increased Exposure Hours," Center Centre UIE, March 30, 2011, *https://oreil.ly/cvfcF*.

your team spends at least a two-hour block of time every six weeks in direct contact with customers. This could be two hours in the call center taking or listening to calls. It could be two hours in the store or on the factory floor watching customers and users. Or it could be doing face-to-face sales of your product in public settings. These activities build empathy, and that in turn drives curiosity. The more curiosity the entire team has about whether or not they are truly meeting customer needs, the greater the likelihood of Lean UX activities ending up on your backlog.

Exploiting the Rhythms of Scrum to Build a Lean UX Practice

Over the years, we've found some useful ways to integrate Lean UX approaches with the rhythms of Scrum. Let's take a look at how you can use Scrum's meeting cadence and Lean UX to build an efficient process.

One approach we put together was to ask teams to map Lean UX activities over a diagram of the Scrum framework to help them bring the integration of the practices into greater focus. We share a typical attempt in Figure 16-4. We think this is a pretty good attempt, but we'd encourage you to try this with your team. As you review it, remember the following caveats:

- This is by no means a comprehensive listing of design activities. There aren't enough Post-its (digital or otherwise) in the world to cover that.
- We use the word Design (often with a capital D) to serve as an umbrella term for all activities that designers of all kinds normally do or take part in.

As with every recommendation in this book, this is a starting point. It shows you how to layer existing activities on top of Scrum. Try it. See what works for you and your team and then adjust based on what you decide during your retrospectives.

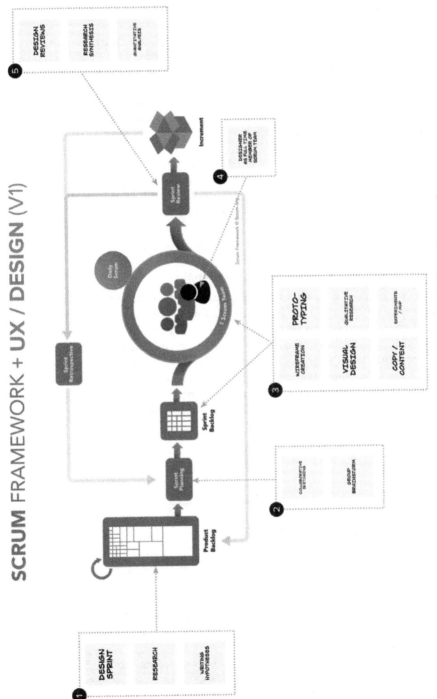

Figure 16-4. *Mapping Lean UX activities to the Scrum framework*

Sprint Goals, Product Goals, and Multi-Sprint Themes

Let's assume your organization has decided on a specific strategic focus for the next two quarters. Your team decides to use a risky hypothesis as the first attempt to achieve the strategy. You can use that hypothesis to create a multi-sprint theme that guides the work you'll do over the next set of sprints. Scrum calls these themes "Product Goals." (Think of a Product Goal as a multi-sprint theme that you use to connect a sequence of sprints.) Your measures of success for your theme are outcomes, as demonstrated in Figure 16-5.

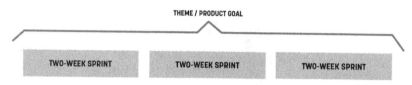

Figure 16-5. *Sprints tied together with a theme or product goal*

Kick off the theme with a collaborative design

Start work on each theme by using the Lean UX Canvas and perhaps a Design Studio exercise.[4] (See Figure 16-6.) Depending on the scope of the hypothesis, the collaborative design session can be as short as an afternoon or as long as a week. You can do them with your immediate team, but you should include a broader group if it's a larger-scale effort. The point of this kickoff is to get the entire team sketching, ideating, and speaking to customers together, creating a backlog of ideas from which to test and learn. In addition, this activity will help define the scope of your theme a bit better—assuming that you've built in some customer feedback loops.

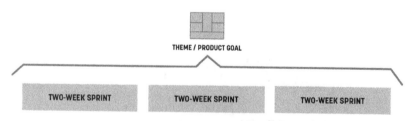

Figure 16-6. *The Lean UX Canvas can capture your sprint theme*

After you've started your regular sprints, you will be testing and validating your ideas: new insights will come in, and you'll need to decide what to do

---

4 You could even use a Google-style "design sprint" here—a confusing name in this context. In this case, we're not advocating for spending a whole sprint doing design. Instead, we're advocating for the process named "design sprint," which we describe in Chapter 14.

with them. You make these decisions by running subsequent shorter brainstorming sessions and collaborative discovery activities as each new sprint begins (Figure 16-7). This allows the team to use the latest insight to create the backlog for the next sprint.

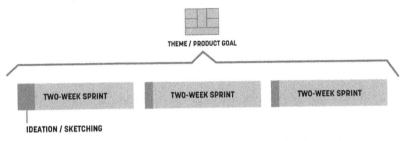

Figure 16-7. *Timing and scope of sketching and ideation sessions*

Sprint planning meeting

Bring your Lean UX Canvas to the sprint planning meeting. Bring the output of your design sprint too. Your mess of sticky notes, sketches, wireframes, paper prototypes, and any other artifacts might seem useless to outside observers but will be meaningful to your team. You made these artifacts together, and because of that you have the shared understanding necessary to extract stories from them. Use them in your planning meeting to write user stories together, and then estimate and prioritize the stories. (See Figure 16-8.)

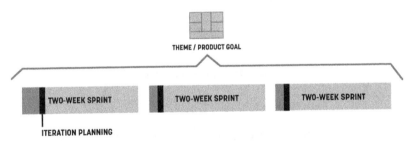

Figure 16-8. *Hold sprint planning meetings immediately after brainstorming sessions*

Experiment stories

As you plan your iteration, there might be additional discovery work that needs to be done during the iteration that wasn't covered in the design sprint or collaborative discovery activities. To accommodate this in your sprint cadence and capture all the work in the same backlog, use experiment stories. Captured by using the same method as your user stories, experiment stories have two distinct benefits:

They visualize discovery work

Discovery work is not inherently tangible as delivery work can be. Experiment stories solve that by leveling the playing field. Everything your team works on—discovery or delivery—goes on the backlog as a story.

They force its prioritization against delivery work:

After those stories are in the backlog, you need to put them in priority order. This forces conversations around *when* to run the experiment and, equally as important, what we *won't* be working on during that same time.

Experiment stories look just like user stories, as illustrated in Figure 16-9.

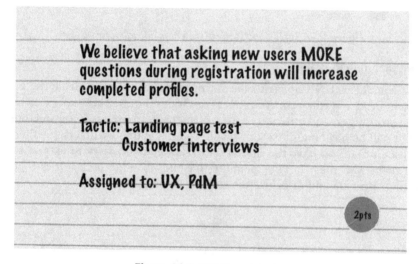

Figure 16-9. *Experiment stories*

Experiment stories contain the following elements:

- The hypothesis you're testing or the thing you're trying to learn
- Tactic(s) for learning (e.g., customer interviews, A/B tests, and prototypes)
- Who will do the work
- A level of effort estimate (if you do estimations) for how much work you expect this to be

After they are written, experiment stories go into your backlog. When their time comes up in the sprint, that's the assigned person's main focus. When the experiment is over, bring the findings to the team immediately and discuss them to determine the impact of these findings. Your team should be ready to change course, even within the current sprint, if the outcome of the experiment stories reveals insights that invalidate your current prioritization.

Pro tip: sometimes we know there will be discovery work to do, but its exact shape or format is unclear at the beginning of a sprint. To ensure the team will have bandwidth for this work during the sprint, place a blank experiment story into your backlog. As the discovery work reveals itself during the sprint, fill it out with details and prioritize appropriately. If it ends up going unused, that's a bit more breathing room your team has during that sprint. Everyone wins.

User validation schedule

Finally, to ensure that you have a constant stream of customer feedback to use for your experiments, plan user research sessions every single week. (See Figure 16-10.) This way your team is never more than five business days away from customer feedback and has ample time to react prior to the end of the sprint. This weekly research cadence provides a good rhythm for your experiment stories and a natural learning point in the sprint.

Use the artifacts you created in the ideation sessions as the base material for your user tests. Remember that when the ideas are raw, you are testing for value. (That is, do people *want to use my product* rather than *can people use my product?*) After you have established that there is a desire for your product, subsequent tests with higher-fidelity artifacts will reveal whether your solution is usable.

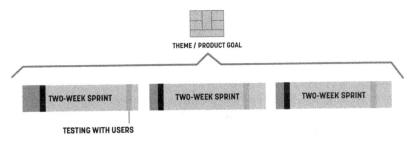

Figure 16-10. *Conversations with users happen during every sprint*

Designers Must Participate in Planning

Agile methods can create a lot of time pressure on designers. Some work fits easily into the context of a user story. Other work needs more time to get it right. Two-week cycles of concurrent development and design offer few opportunities for designers to ruminate on big problems. And although some Agile methods take a more flexible approach to time than Scrum does (for example, Kanban does away with the notion of a two-week batch of work and places the emphasis on continuous flow), most designers feel pressure to fit their work into the time box of the sprint. For this reason, designers need to participate in the sprint planning process.

The major reason designers feel pressure in Agile processes is that they don't (for whatever reason) fully participate in the process. This is typically not their fault: when Agile is understood as simply a way to build software, there doesn't appear to be any reason to include nontechnologists in the process. However, without designer participation, their concerns and needs are not taken into account in project plans. As a result, many Agile teams don't make plans that allow designers to do their best work.

For Lean UX to work, the entire team must participate in all activities—stand-ups, retrospectives, planning meetings, brainstorming sessions—as a normal rule, they all require everyone's attendance to be successful. Besides negotiating the complexity of certain features, cross-functional participation allows designers and developers to create effective backlog prioritization.

For example, imagine at the beginning of a sprint that the first story a team prioritizes has a heavy design component to it. Imagine that the designer was not there to voice their concern. That team will fail as soon as they meet for their stand-up the next day. The designer will call out that the story has not been designed. The designer will say that it will take at least two to three days to complete the design before the story is ready for development. Imagine instead that the designer had participated in the prioritization of the backlog. Their concern would have been raised at planning time. The team could have selected a story card that needed less design preparation to work on first—which would have bought the designer the time they needed to complete the work.

The other casualty of sparse participation is shared understanding. Teams make decisions in meetings. Those decisions are based on discussions. Even if 90% of a meeting is not relevant to your immediate need, the 10% that is relevant will save hours of time downstream. Participation gives you the ability to negotiate for the time you need to do your work. This is true for UX designers as much as it is for everyone else on the team.

Stakeholders and the Risks Dashboard

Management check-ins are one of the biggest obstacles to maintaining team momentum. Designers are used to doing design reviews, but unfortunately, check-ins don't end there. Product owners, stakeholders, CEOs, and clients all want to know how things are going. They all want to bless the project plan going forward. The challenge for outcome-focused teams is that their project plans are dependent on what they are learning. They are responsive, so their typical plan lays out only small batches of work at a time. At most, these teams plan an iteration or two ahead. This perceived "short-sightedness" tends not to satisfy most high-level managers, which can lead to micromanagement. How then do you keep the check-ins under control while maintaining the pace of your Lean UX and Scrum processes?

Two words: *proactive communication.*

Jeff once managed a team that radically altered the workflow for an existing product that had thousands of paying customers. The team was so excited by the changes they'd made that they went ahead with the launch without alerting anyone else in the organization. Within an hour of the new product going live, the vice president of customer service was at Jeff's desk, fuming and demanding to know why she wasn't told of this change. The issue was this: when customers have problems with the product, they call in for help. Call center representatives use scripts to troubleshoot customer problems and to offer solutions —except they didn't have a script for this new product. Because they didn't know it was going to change.

This healthy slice of humble pie served as a valuable lesson. If you want your stakeholders—both those managing you and those dependent on you—to stay out of your way, make sure that they are aware of your plans and your progress. While working together at our agency Neo, our colleague Nicole Rufuku came up with a remarkably simple and powerful tool for doing just this: the Risks Dashboard (Figure 16-11).

RISKS DASHBOARD

Users may not value our service enough to pay for subscription.	Trending positive	Price testing underway.
Users may need our service only occasionally.	Not enough data	Longitudinal tracking data study in progress.
Users may be confused by our branding.	TBD	To be evaluated.
Users may be too embarrassed to seek out our service.	TBD	Testing scheduled for next week.
Technical risk: we may not have enough data to evaluate each case.	Trending positive	Technical pilot trending positive.
Regulatory risk: we may be relying on illegal data.	Trending positive	In conversation with Regulators.

Figure 16-11. *The Risks Dashboard*

The Risks Dashboard is nothing more than a three-column chart you can create in PowerPoint, Excel, or Google Docs.

- The first column lists the major outstanding risks associated with your current initiative. These are things that are critical to the success of the product.

- The middle column has a scale of how severe this risk might be and a color-coded display of how that risk is trending. Is it something that might require a small fix? Or is it existential to the success of the product? Is our discovery work telling us that this is increasingly possible or not as bad as we thought?

- The third column tells what we're doing about that risk.

This dashboard is a living document that you use to communicate with your stakeholders and clients about the status of your project. Use this dashboard in your planning meetings with your team. Use it in your sprint demos with your stakeholders to help drive important decisions. In doing so, you are informing your stakeholders about:

- How the work is progressing
- What you have learned so far
- What risk you'll focus on next
- Outcomes (how you're trending toward your goal) not feature sets
- Dependent departments (customer service, marketing, operations, etc.) and their need to be aware of upcoming changes that can affect them

Often there will be a risk in the dashboard where the third column is empty. A stakeholder will then ask why we're not doing anything about this risk. Sometimes this is simply a matter of prioritization. But sometimes you may be blocked on progress. So a stakeholder question gives you a perfect opportunity to bring up any challenges you may have in doing discovery work, prioritizing it, or getting budget or approval to do it. With the Risks Dashboard, you are effectively contextualizing the discovery with business impact. Business impact tends to resonate powerfully with stakeholders, which makes this an effective tool to drive a better integration of your Lean UX work with your Agile delivery process.

Outcome-Based Road Maps

One of the biggest challenges in Agile is planning the work in a linear, visual way. Sure, we've had "road maps" for a long time, but they don't do a great job of representing the true nature of software development. Digital product development is not linear. It is iterative. We build some things. We ship them. We see how they impact customer behavior. We iterate them and ship again.

The traditional linear road map model—one where there is a starting point and a clear, feature-specific end point (almost always with a fixed date)—is outdated. It reflects an output-focused mode of operating a digital business. Instead, as we've discussed throughout this book, successful product-led organizations focus on outcomes. How then do we build product road maps in a world of continuous improvement, learning, and agility? And how can this type of visualization ensure that Lean UX takes place in our Agile process? We use outcome-based road maps.

Here is what an Agile product road map should look like (Figure 16-12).

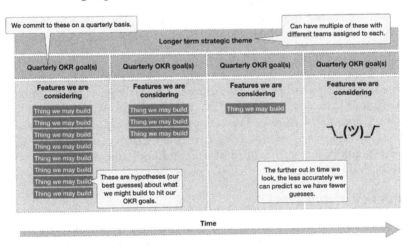

Figure 16-12. *An Agile product road map*

You'll notice a few key components in this diagram:

Strategic themes

These are the organizational product strategies set by executive leaders that point teams in a specific direction. These can be things like "Expand our market share in Europe" or "Leverage the under-utilized time our fleet isn't ferrying passengers to deliver other goods and food." There can be multiple themes running in parallel for a larger organization.

Quarterly OKR goals

OKRs, when done well, use customer behavior as the metrics in the "key results" part of the equation. These quarterly outcome goals are where each team is going to focus in an effort to help achieve the strategic theme. This is the goal teams strive to achieve. It is their definition of success and their *real* definition of done. Teams should work together with leadership to ensure these are aligned and properly levelled.

Feature/product hypotheses

These are each team's best guesses as to how they will achieve this quarter's OKR goals. Looking one quarter in advance, a team can make strong, well-educated guesses about what product or feature ideas they think will achieve their quarterly goals. Looking out two quarters ahead, those guesses become less confident, so teams will make fewer guesses and fewer commitments. Looking three and four quarters out, the teams really have no idea what they'll be working on, so these guesses become fewer and fewer. This is exactly the way it should be. Teams will learn in the next quarter or two how well their ideas worked, what moves the needles forward, and what their next guesses should be. The boxes for Q3 and Q4 will fill up as learning from Q1 and Q2 gets synthesized and acted on.

Visualizing work this way immediately puts the uncertainty of software development front and center in the conversation. When stakeholders ask, "How will we determine whether these are the right hypotheses to work on now and in the future?" the answer is Lean UX. Your team will work to build learning into every sprint to ensure you're always working toward the strategic theme and not wasting time on initiatives that don't bring you closer. Couple that with the Agile cadences described above, and you have a powerful recipe for delivering valuable experiences to your customers.

Frequency of Review

Each team should present this type of outcome-based road map for review at the beginning of an annual cycle. It should align with the strategic goals leadership has set and ensure their OKRs use metrics that ladder up to these goals.

While it's incumbent on the team to continually expose what they are doing, learning, and deciding, official check-ins should happen on a quarterly basis. Teams meet with leaders to determine how well they've tracked toward their outcome goals, what they've learned during the last quarter, and what they plan on doing in the next quarter. This is a perfect opportunity to reaffirm the validity of the team's goals going forward and to make any adjustments based on new learnings, market conditions, or any other factor that may have affected the direction of the company.

Measuring Progress

It should be clear by now that progress on this type of road map is not measured in how many features have been delivered or whether they've been delivered on time. Instead, progress is measured in terms of how well we've changed customer behavior for the better. If our ideas didn't drive customer success, we kill those ideas and move on to new ones. The learning drives ideas for future quarterly backlogs. It also drives our agility as a team and as a business.

These road maps are living documents. We don't fix these at the beginning of an annual cycle and leave them as if they were etched in stone. There is too much uncertainty and complexity in delivering digital products and services. Product-led organizations—those focused on customer success with empowered teams—work to make sure that they're always pointed in the right direction. This means adjusting road maps as the reality on the ground changes. Outcome-based road maps ensure that leaders and teams are being transparent with each other, realistic about their goals, and most importantly realistic about how they measure success.

Lean UX and Agile in the Enterprise

Many of the tactics covered in this book are focused on one team. But in the real world, large organizations have multiple product development teams working in parallel. How does Lean UX scale when the number of teams grows to tens or even hundreds of concurrent workstreams?

This is one version of the scaling question—which is itself an ongoing question in the Agile community. As Lean and Agile methods have become the default ways of working, many people have become focused on this question. Large organizations have a legitimate need to coordinate the activity of multiple teams, and processes that embrace uncertainty and embrace *learning-your-way-forward* present a challenge to most traditional project management methods.

Let's address the elephant in the room—the Scaled Agile Framework or SAFe. As of this writing, SAFe has been around for 10 years, and for many large organizations, it's the first choice for implementing a whole-organization approach to agility. If you're not familiar with it, SAFe is a comprehensive, detailed, hierarchical set of processes, diagrams, and vocabulary that are all designed to increase the agility of large organizations. It works in a top-down way to divide and delegate the work to "Agile Release Trains" who follow a rigid release schedule. Unfortunately, these processes are largely devoid of user feedback or learning.

You might have been as surprised, as we were, to learn that version 4.5 of the SAFe framework included Lean UX. Because of this, we get many questions about how to do Lean UX in a company that has implemented SAFe. The short answer is this: you can't. SAFe is designed for production, not for discovery. It is optimized to ensure a continuous flow of output and minimize change requirements on executives. It creates a rigidity within the software development process that results in something that can't, in any real way, be described as agile.

SAFe Is Not Agile

Ever since the Scaled Agile Framework (SAFe for short) adopted Lean UX in version 4.5, we've received a steady stream of inbound questions about how, exactly, these two methods are supposed to work well together.

The short answer is, we have no idea.

The slightly longer answer is that all the principles we've built into Lean UX don't seem to exist in SAFe.

Continuous learning and improvement, customer centricity, humility, cross-functional collaboration, evidence-based decision making, experimentation, design, and course correction—to name a few—are visibly absent from the SAFe conversation. Instead, organizations adopting this way of working focus on rigid team structures, strict rituals and events, and an uneven distribution of behavior change requirements depending on how high up one sits in the organization.

In short, SAFe is not agile.

Given the heavy training regimen teams have to go through to become "SAFe certified," it's no wonder they resist change. They've been trained to work in a very specific way—a way focused solely on predictable delivery, not learning, not course correction, and certainly not agility. The activities that make teams truly agile require flexibility in planning. They require alignment on customer success, not a predetermined set of features. They require a continuous discovery process that inevitably leads to unplanned course corrections. These corrections would "derail" a Release Train in no time.

Large organizations seeking agility realize the uncertainty that comes with it and cling to the familiarity of waterfall processes. SAFe gives the illusion of "adopting agile" while allowing familiar management processes to remain intact. In a world of rapid continuous change, evolving consumer consumption patterns, geopolitical instability, and exponential technological advancements, this way of working is unsustainable.

If you work in a large organization that has adopted or is in the process of implementing SAFe, ask yourself what's changed during this transition. Are you closer to your customers? How long does it take to learn whether you've delivered something of value? Even better, how are you measuring "value"? Ask yourself how easy it would be to pivot an initiative based on a new discovery? Then compare those answers to how things were before you started using terms like "big room planning," "PI," and "release train engineer."

> Scaling any way of working in a large organization is tricky and uneven. Attempting to apply one blanket process to the entire company—a process that is focused strictly on delivery rather than continuous discovery and course correction—only hardens traditional ways of working. SAFe is compelling because it seems to offer a one-size-fits-all recipe for agility at scale. In reality, it rewards predictability, conformity, and compliance while providing executives with cover for the question "How do we become more agile?"

A full discussion of how to create a truly Agile and Lean organization is beyond the scope of this book.[5] And honestly, it's a hard problem with few easy answers. It requires leadership to radically rethink the way it sets strategy, assembles teams, and plans and assigns work. In essence, organizations need to reduce the amount of scaffolding they put in place and allow teams to organically find ways to use the basic values, principles, and methods of small-team Agile to build a productive working cadence and then scale those organization-specific approaches in small increments.

That said, there are a few techniques that can help Lean UX scale in enterprise Agile environments and even take advantage of that scale. Here are just a few issues that typically arise and ways to manage for them.

Issue: projects grow bigger, more teams are assigned to them. How do you ensure that all teams are aligned to the same vision and not optimizing locally?

Solution approach: The concept of managing with outcomes applies to a set of teams as much as it does to individual ones. To ensure that all the teams working on the same project have a shared vision, assign them all the same success metric, expressed as an outcome. Working together, they can define the leading indicators that drive that metric and divide those leading metrics between the teams on the project. But teams must not be allowed to focus on leading metrics to the exclusion of the larger outcome: the entire set of teams succeeds only if they hit the overarching outcome together.

Working together this way reduces the risk of local optimization with disregard for follow-on impacts of that optimization. For example, if the marketing team is working to hit their acquisition outcomes goals but overutilize email to achieve that goal, it may hurt the product team's retention goal. If both of these teams had the same outcome goals—a mix of acquisition and retention—they would work together to learn how to balance their efforts and outputs to be successful.

---

5 We've written a high-level overview of this subject in our book *Sense & Respond* (Harvard Business Review Press, 2017). (See *https://senseandrespond.co*.)

Issue: How do you ensure that teams are sharing what they're learning and minimizing duplicate effort to learn the same things?

Solution approach: Although there's no silver bullet to solve for this issue, the successful practices we've seen include a central knowledge management tool (like a wiki), regular team leadership meetings (like a Scrum of Scrums), and open-communication tools that focus on research (like a dedicated channel on Slack or your internal chat tool). Elements from studio culture, like regular cross-team critique sessions, can help too.

Issue: Cross-team dependencies can keep progress at a crawl. How do you maintain a regular pace of learning and delivery in a multiteam environment?

Solution approach: Create self-sufficient "full-stack" teams. Full-stack teams have every capability needed for them to do their work on the team. This doesn't mean that they need a person from each department—just that there is someone on the team who can do one or more of the things the team might need. The specific disciplines on the team—designers, content people, frontend developers, backend developers, product managers—coordinate with one another at discipline-specific meetings to ensure that they are up to date on their practice, but the work takes place locally.

Wrapping Up

This chapter took a detailed look at how Lean UX fits into an Agile process. In addition, we looked at how cross-functional collaboration allows a team to move forward at a brisk pace, and how to handle stakeholders and managers who always want to know what's going on. We discussed why having everyone participate in all activities is critical and how the staggered-sprint model, once considered the path to true agility, formed the roots of dual-track Agile, which is now the new target model for most teams. We also covered, in detail, how scrum artifacts and events work to your advantage in building up your velocity of learning.

PART IV

LEAN UX IN YOUR ORGANIZATION

About Part IV

Integrating design into Agile is never easy. Sometimes it causes a lot of pain and heartache. Jeff learned that firsthand when he was at TheLadders. After spending some time trying to integrate UX work with an Agile process, Jeff was feeling pretty good—until one morning his UX team delivered the diagram below (Figure IV-1). This diagram visualized all of the challenges the team was facing as they tried to integrate their practice into Agile. It served initially as a large slice of humble pie. Ultimately, though, it provided the beginning of conversations that helped Jeff, his UX team, and the rest of TheLadders' product development staff build an integrated, collaborative practice.

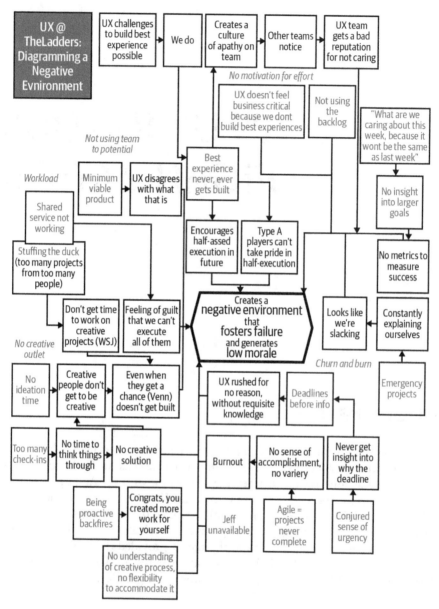

Figure IV-1. *The UX team at TheLadders expressed their feelings about our Agile/UX integration efforts*

In the years since this diagram was created, we've been fortunate to work with lots of companies on this challenge. We've worked with companies that spanned a broad range of industries, company sizes, and cultures. We've helped media organizations figure out new ways to deliver and monetize their content. We've built new, mobile-first sales tools for a commercial furniture manufacturer. We've consulted with fashion retailers, automotive services companies, and large banks to help them build Lean UX practices. We've worked with nonprofits to create new service offerings. And we've trained countless teams.

Each of these projects provided us a bit more insight into how Lean UX works in that environment. We used that insight to make each subsequent project that much more successful. We've built up a body of knowledge over the past five years that has given us a clear sense of what needs to happen—at the team and at the organization level—for Lean UX to succeed. That is the focus of Section IV.

In Chapter 17, "Making Organizational Shifts", we'll dig into the specific organizational changes that need to be made to support this way of working. It's not just software developers and designers who need to find a way to work together. Your whole product development engine is going to need to change if you want to create a truly Agile organization.

In Chapter 18, "Lean UX in an Agency", we'll discuss the issues that are unique to implementing Lean UX in an agency context. Having lived this challenge ourselves, and worked to train any number of design and product-development firms, we've come to understand some of the challenges here. We'll share some of the key things you'll need to consider to make Lean UX successful in this kind of business.

CHAPTER 17

Making Organizational Shifts

In baseball, you don't know nothing.
Yogi Berra

In Part I of this book, we discussed the principles behind Lean UX. We hope you understand from that section that Lean UX is a mindset. In Part II, we discussed some of the key methods of Lean UX, because Lean UX is also a process. As we've worked with clients and taught these methods to teams, it's become clear that Lean UX is also an operational and management method. For this reason, you'll need to make some changes in your organization to get the most benefit from working this way.

Organizational shifts aren't easy, but they're not optional. The world has changed: our organizations must change with it. Any business of scale (or any business that seeks to scale) is, like it or not, in the software business. Regardless of the industry in which your company operates, software has become central to delivering your product or service.

This is both empowering and threatening. The ability to reach global markets, scale operations to meet increased demand, and create a continuous conversation with your customers has never been easier. This power is also a double-edged sword: it offers these same opportunities to smaller competitors who would never have been able to compete before the broad adoption of software. This makes the need to adopt Lean UX all the more urgent.

Many organizations have come to this conclusion and, in response, have sought to scale their product development teams. As they've done so, many have used the core rhythms of Agile software development techniques to operationalize software product development. Unfortunately, many of these approaches are agile in name only. They fail to adopt the key values of Agile, which include collaboration, transparency, and continuous learning These operational approaches maximize delivery velocity but force software teams—including the designers on these teams—into production mode. As a result, much of the value of design gets lost.

Lean UX is a way to break out of design-as-production and realize the full value of design on cross-functional teams. It makes it possible for you to use the power of software to create a continuous improvement loop that allows your company to stay ahead of its competitors. It's this loop that drives real organizational agility and allows your company to react to changes in the market at speeds never before possible.

DesignOps and Lean UX

As large organizations have embraced design in the operational context of product development teams, we've seen the rise of a movement called DesignOps. DesignOps has as its goal simply the operationalizing of design at scale. It's a way of thinking about and managing the operations of design inside large organizations. This means that the DesignOps team in your organization must become key players in any effort to adopt Lean UX.

One important callout here: DesignOps can be a force for embracing new ways of working, but it can also be a force for embracing legacy ways of working. Many of the traditional ways of working that the design community has developed are wonderful, full of wisdom, and need to be honored. But some ways of working are very specific to the design work we did with older technologies and older business models. BDUF (Big Design Up Front) and deliverable-based work are just two examples of traditional time-honored design methods that no longer serve the best interests of designers who are seeking maximum impact on Agile teams. As you work to forge a DesignOps-led movement in your organization, beware of "designers have always done it this way" solutions, which do not embrace the true spirit of Agile and Lean UX.

The Shifts

When we train teams, they sometimes ask, "How can we put these methods into practice here?" And on this point, we're always a little hesitant. Although we're confident that most organizations can solve these problems, we're also aware that every organization is different. Finding the right solution requires a lot of close work and collaboration with your colleagues and your executives.

To prepare you for that work, we're going to use this chapter to share some of the shifts that organizations need to make in order to embrace Lean UX. We're not going to tell you *how* to make those shifts; that's your job. But we hope this discussion will help you survey the landscape to find the areas you're going to want to address.

Changing Culture

As you implement Lean UX, consider these dimensions of culture:

- Be humble.
- Embrace new skills.
- Create open, collaborative workspaces.
- No heroes.
- Fall in love with the problem, not the solution.
- Evolve agency culture.
- Be realistic about your environment.

Shifting Team Organization

To implement Lean UX, you'll also need to rethink the way you organize teams:

- Think competencies over roles.
- Create cross-functional teams.
- Create small teams.
- Work with distributed teams.
- Build flexibility into third-party vendor relationships.

Shifting Process

Finally, your product development processes will change as well:

- Plan work using outcomes, not output.
- Beware of BDUF sneaking into Agile environments.
- Embrace speed first, aesthetics second,
- Tackle UX debt.
- Rethink documentation practices.
- Manage up and out.

Shift: Be humble

Imagine for a moment that you work on an assembly line that makes cars. The end state of your product is well-defined in advance. The cost of producing that product is clear. The process to create it has been optimized, and the ways customers will use that car—based on more than one hundred years of observation—is also clear. In situations like this, the focus is on quality, efficiency, and cost control.

We're not building cars.

Our medium is software, and our products and services are complex and unpredictable. They don't have an end state. We can continue to design, build, operate, and optimize our digital products as long as it makes economic sense to do so. Most perplexing is that our customers might use our digital services in ways we never imagined. In many cases, the best features of a system emerge over time as people use the system. (Twitter's hashtag is a great example of this: users invented this feature, and then Twitter added support for it after the fact.) With so many unknowns, there is only so much confidence we can have in the scope, road map, implementation, and success of our product. The good news is that through the rise of the Agile and DevOps movements, we can move away from the assembly-line methods of past generations and adopt continuous production methods. When we pair that capability with Lean UX, we get the ability to learn very quickly how valid or invalid our ideas are.

To fully take advantage of these new capabilities, your organization must embrace humility. Your organization must accept that, in the face of all this complexity and uncertainty, we just can't predict the exact shape our service will have to take to be successful. This is not an abdication of vision.

Instead, it requires a strong opinion about the shape the system should take, coupled with the willingness to change course if evidence from the market reveals that initial vision was wrong. Adopting this mindset makes it safe for teams to experiment, fail, and learn. It is only through this trial-and-error process that Lean UX can thrive. If the organization doesn't make room for course correction, the continuous learning that Lean UX promotes will be seen, at best, as a distraction and, at worst, as a waste of time.

Shift: Embrace new skills

Many companies turn to designers for the most tactical and traditional capabilities: wireframing, specification, UI design, etc. They limit their participation in a project to the "design phase" of whatever process the company happens to be using. Plugging designers into these existing workflows limits their effectiveness by limiting the scope of their work, which has a side effect of reinforcing a siloed team model.

The success of a collaborative team demands more. Although teams still need core UX skills, designers must add facilitation as one of their core competencies. This requires two significant shifts to the way we've worked to date:

Designers must open up the design process
> The team—not the individual—needs to own the product design. Instead of hiding behind a monitor for days at a time, designers need to bring their teams into the design process, seek their input, and build that insight into the design. Doing so will begin to break down silos and promote a more cross-functional conversation to take place. To do this, designers must employ a broad range of collaborative tactics and must be both creative and deeply practical—seeking tactics that meet the team's needs, advance the conversation, and respect the realities of team capacity and project timeline.

Designers must take a leadership role on their team
> Your colleagues are used to giving you critique on your design work. What they're not used to doing is cocreating that design with you. Design leadership and facilitation in group brainstorming activities like Design Studio can create safe forums for the entire team to conceptualize your product and showcase the synthesizing capabilities of the design team.

Shift: Create open, collaborative workspaces

Break down the physical barriers that prevent collaboration. Colocate your teams and create workspaces for them that keep everyone visible and accessible. Make space for your team to put their work up on walls and other work surfaces. Nothing is more effective than walking over to a colleague, showing some work, discussing, sketching, exchanging ideas, understanding facial expressions and body language, and reaching a resolution on a thorny topic.

When you colocate people, create cross-functional groupings. That means removing them from the comforts of their discipline's "hideout." It's amazing how even one cubicle wall can hinder conversation between colleagues.

Open workspaces make it possible for team members to see each other and to easily reach out when questions arise. Some teams have gone as far as putting their desks on wheels so that they can relocate closer to the team members they're collaborating with on that particular day. Augment these open spaces with breakout rooms where the teams can brainstorm. Wall-sized whiteboards or simply painting the walls with whiteboard paint provides many square feet of discussion space. In short, remove the physical obstacles between your team members. Your space planners might not like it at first, but your stakeholders will thank you.

As distributed teams and "hybrid" work situations become more common, remember to carry over these qualities to these situations as well. Ensure that collaboration and sharing are easy and that your teams have the tools that make them most successful rather than the ones IT has chosen for them.

Shift: No heroes

As we've continued to work with a wider variety of teams, there are still many designers who resist Lean UX. One reason? Many designers want to be heroes.

In an environment in which designers create beautiful deliverables, they can maintain a heroic aura. Requirements go in one end of the design machine, and gorgeous artwork makes its way out. People "ooh" and "aah" when the design is unveiled. Designers have thrived on these reactions (both informal and formalized as awards) for many years.

We're not suggesting that all of these designs are superficial. Schooling, formal training, experience, and a healthy dose of inspiration go into every photoshop document that designers create—and often the results are smart, well considered, and valuable. However, those glossy deliverables can drive bad corporate decisions—they can bias judgment specifically because their beauty is so persuasive. Awards can be based on the aesthetics of the designs (rather than the outcome the design creates). Hiring decisions are made on the sharpness of wireframes, and compensation can depend on the brand names attached to each of the portfolio pieces.

The result of this is that the creators of these documents are heralded as thought leaders and elevated to the top of the experience design field. They are recognized as the "go-to" people when the problem has to get solved quickly. But can a single design hero be responsible for the success of the user experience, the business, and the team? Should one person be heralded as the sole reason for an initiative's success?

In short, no.

For Lean UX to succeed in your organization, all types of contributors— designers and nondesigners—need to collaborate broadly. This can be a hard shift for some, especially for visual designers with a background in interactive agencies. In those contexts, the creative director is untouchable. In Lean UX, the only thing that's untouchable is customer insight.

Lean UX literally has no time for heroes. The entire concept of design as hypothesis immediately dethrones notions of heroism; as a designer, you must expect that many of your ideas will fail in testing. Heroes don't admit failure. But Lean UX designers embrace it as part of the process.

Shift: Fall in love with the problem, not the solution

Lean UX makes us ask hard questions about the nature of quality in our design work.

If you're a designer reading this, you've probably asked yourself a question that often comes up when speed trumps aesthetic perfection:

> If my job is now to put out concepts and ideas instead of finished work, everything I produce will feel half-assed. I feel like I'm "going for the bronze." Nothing I produce will ever be finished. Nothing is indicative of the kind of products I am capable of designing. How can I feel pride and ownership for designs that are simply not done?

For some designers, Lean UX threatens what they value in their work and puts their portfolio at risk. It might even feel as though it threatens their future employability. These emotions are based on what many hiring managers have valued to date—sexy deliverables (i.e., solutions). Rough sketches, "version one" of a project, and other low-fidelity artifacts are not the making of a "killer portfolio." With the realization that software solutions continue to evolve over time, all of that is now changing.

Although your organization must continue to value aesthetics, polish, and attention to detail, other dimensions of design are equally important. The ability to understand the context of a business problem, think fast, and build shared understanding needs to get a promotion. Designers can demonstrate their problem-solving skills by illustrating the paths they took to get from idea to validated learning to experience. In doing so, they'll demonstrate their deep worth as designers. Organizations that seek out and reward problem-solvers will attract—and be attracted to—these designers.

Shift: Evolve agency culture

Applying Lean UX in a digital agency is no small challenge. Most agencies have a business model that conflicts with Lean UX. The traditional agency business model is simple: clients pay for deliverables—designs, specs, code, PowerPoint decks—not outcomes. But agency culture is also a huge obstacle. The culture of hero design is strong in places that elevate individuals to positions like executive creative director. Cross-disciplinary collaboration can also be difficult in big agencies, where the need to keep utilization high has led to processes that encourage functional silos. These, in turn, lead to "project phases" that encourage deliverable-centric work.

Perhaps the most challenging obstacle is the client's expectation to "throw it over the wall" to the agency and then see the results when they're ready. Collaboration between client and agency in these situations can be limited to uninformed and unproductive critique that is based on personal bias, politics, and ass-covering.

To make Lean UX work in an agency, everyone involved in an engagement must focus on maximizing two factors: increasing collaboration between client and agency, and working to change the focus from outputs to outcomes.

Some agencies are attempting to focus on outcomes by experimenting with a move away from fixed-scope and deliverable-based contracts. Instead, their engagements are based on simple time-and-materials agreements or, more radically, on outcome-based contracts. In either case, teams become freer to spend their time iterating toward a goal. Clients give up the illusion of control that a deliverables-based contract offers but gain a freedom to pursue meaningful and high-quality solutions that are defined in terms of outcomes, not feature lists.

To increase collaboration, agencies can try to break down the walls that separate them from their clients. Clients can be pulled into the process earlier and more frequently. Check-ins can be constructed around less formal milestones. And collaborative work sessions can be arranged so that both agency and client benefit from the additional insight, feedback, and collaboration with each other.

These are not easy transformations—either for the agency or the client who hires them—but it is the model under which the best products are built.

A quick note about development partners. In agency relationships, software development teams (either at the agency, at the client, or working as a third party) are often treated as outsiders and often brought in at the end of a design phase. It's imperative that you change this: development partners must participate through the life of the project—and not simply as passive observers. Instead, you should seek to have software development begin as early as possible. Again, you are looking to create a deep and meaningful collaboration with the entire project team—and to do that, you must actually be working side by side with the developers.

Shift: Be realistic about your environment

Change is scary. The Lean UX approach brings with it a lot of change. This can be especially disconcerting for managers who have been in their positions for a while and are comfortable in their current roles. Some managers can be threatened by proposals to work in a new way—which could end up having negative consequences for you. In these situations, try asking for forgiveness rather than permission. Try out some ideas and prove their value with quantifiable success. Whether you saved time and money on the project or put out a more successful update than ever before, these achievements can help make your case. If your manager still doesn't see the value in working this way and you believe your organization is progressing down a path of continued "blind design," perhaps it's time to consider alternative employment.

Shift: Think competencies over roles

In most companies, the work you do is determined by your job title. That job title comes with a job description. Too often, people in organizations discourage others from working outside the confines of their job descriptions (e.g., "You're not a developer, what can you possibly know about JavaScript?"). This approach is deeply anticollaborative and leaves people's full set of skills, talents, and competencies unused.

Discouraging cross-functional input encourages organizational silos. The more discrete a person's job is, the easier it becomes to retreat to the safe confines of that discipline. As a result, conversation across disciplines wanes, and mistrust, finger-pointing, and CYA ("cover your ass") behavior grows.

Silos are the death of collaborative teams.

For Lean UX to succeed, your organization needs to adopt a mantra of "competencies over roles." Every team member possesses a core competency—design, software development, research, and so on—and must deliver on that skill set. However, members might also possess secondary competencies that make the team work more efficiently.

Allow your colleagues to contribute to any disciplines in which they have expertise and interest. You'll find it creates a more engaged team that can complete tasks more efficiently. You'll also find it builds camaraderie across job titles as people with different disciplines show interest in what their colleagues are doing. Teams that enjoy working together produce better work.

Shift: Create cross-functional teams

For many teams, collaboration is a single-discipline activity. Developers solve problems with other developers while designers go sit on bean bags, fire up the lava lamps, and "ideate" with their black-turtlenecked brethren. (We kid.) (Well...only a little. We love designers.)

The ideas born of single-discipline collaborations are single faceted. They don't reflect the broader perspective of the team, which can illuminate a wider range of needs, opportunities, risks, and solutions. Worse, working this way requires discipline-based teams to explain their work. Too often, the result is a heavy reliance on detailed documentation and a slowdown in the broader team's learning pace.

Lean UX requires cross-functional collaboration. By creating interaction among product managers, developers, QA engineers, designers, and marketers, you put everyone on the same page. Equally important: you put everyone on the same level. No single discipline dictates to the other. All are working toward a common goal. Allow your designers to attend "developer meetings" and vice versa. In fact, just have team meetings.

We've known how important cross-functional collaboration is for a long time. Robert Dailey's study from the late '70s called "The Role of Team and Task Characteristics in R&D Team Collaborative Problem Solving and Productivity" found a link between a team's problem-solving productivity and what he called "four predictors," which included "task certainty, task interdependence, team size, and team cohesiveness."[1]

Keep your team cohesive by breaking down the discipline-based boundaries.

Shift: Create small teams

Larger groups of people are less efficient than smaller ones. This makes intuitive sense. But less obvious is this: a smaller team must work on smaller problems. This small size makes it easier to maintain the discipline needed to produce minimum viable products (MVPs). Break your big teams into what Amazon founder Jeff Bezos famously called "two-pizza teams." If the team needs more than two pizzas to make a meal, it's too big.

If the task is large, break it down into related pieces of work that several small teams can handle simultaneously. Align those teams with a single outcome to achieve. This way, all of them are working toward the same goal. This forces these small teams to self-organize and communicate efficiently while reducing the risk of each team optimizing locally.

Shift: Work with distributed teams

As the COVID-19 pandemic has shown us, colocation is not always an option. When setting up distributed teams, give them the tools they need to communicate and collaborate. These include things like videoconferencing software (e.g., Zoom), real-time communication services (e.g., Slack), online whiteboard tools (e.g., Mural and Miro), simple file-sharing software (e.g., Dropbox, Google Docs), remote-pairing software (e.g., Screenhero), and anything else that might make their collaboration easier and more productive.

When it's possible to travel, don't forget that occasionally plane tickets to meet each other in the flesh go a long way toward maintaining long-distance collaboration. Perhaps the most important thing to remember if you're trying to implement Lean UX with distributed teams is this: the members of these teams

---

1 Robert C. Daley, "The Role of Team and Task Characteristics in R&D Team Collaborative Problem Solving and Productivity," *Management Science* 24, no. 15 (November 1, 1978): 1557–1676, *https://oreil.ly/hnN7a*.

must be awake at the same time. The overlap doesn't need to cover an entire workday, but there must be some block of time every day during which colleagues can have conversations and participate in collaborative exercises.

Shift: Build flexibility into third-party vendor relationships

Third-party software development vendors pose a big challenge to Lean UX methods. If a portion of your work is outsourced to a third-party vendor—regardless of the location of the vendor—the Lean UX process is more likely to break down. This is because the contractual relationship with these vendors can make the flexibility that Lean UX requires difficult to achieve.

When working with third-party vendors, try to create projects based on time and materials. This will make it possible for you to create a flexible relationship with your development partner. You will need this in order to respond to the changes that are part of the Lean UX process. Remember, you are building software to learn, and that learning will cause your plans to change. Plan for that change and structure your vendor relationships around it.

When selecting partners, remember that many outsourced development shops are oriented toward production work and see rework as a problem rather than a learning opportunity. When seeking partners for Lean UX work, look for teams willing to embrace experimentation and iteration and who clearly understand the difference between prototyping-to-learn and developing-for-production.

Shift: Plan work using outcomes, not output

Chapter 3 discusses the role of outcomes in Lean UX. Lean UX teams measure their success not in terms of completed features but in terms of progress toward specific outcomes. Determining outcomes is a leadership activity; it's one that many organizations are not good at or don't do at all. Too often, leadership directs the product team through a feature-centric product road map—a set of outputs and features that they require the product team to produce by a specific date.

Teams using Lean UX must be empowered to decide for themselves which features will create the outcomes their organizations require. To do this, teams must shift their conversation with leadership from one based on features to one centered on outcomes. This conversational shift is a radical one. Product managers must determine which business metrics require the most attention. What effect are they trying to create? Are they trying to influence customer behavior? If so, how? Are they trying to increase performance? If so, by what measure? These metrics must be linked to a larger business impact.

Leadership must set this direction. If not, teams must demand this shift of them. Teams must ask, "Why are we working on this project?" and "How will we know we've done a good job?" Managers need to be retrained to give their teams the answers to these questions. They must be given the freedom to work with their teams to determine which features best achieve these goals. Teams must move from feature road maps to backlogs of hypotheses to test. Work should be prioritized based on risk, feasibility, and potential success.

Shift: Beware of BDUF sneaking into Agile environments

In the Agile community, you sometimes hear people talk about Big Design Up Front or BDUF. We've been advocating moving away from BDUF for years. But it wasn't always that way.

In the early 2000s, Jeff was a UI designer at AOL, working on a new browser. The team was working on coming up with ways to innovate on existing browser feature sets. But they always had to wait to implement anything until Jeff created the appropriate mock-ups, specifications, and flow diagrams that described these new ideas.

One developer got tired of waiting and started implementing some of these ideas before the documents were complete. Jeff was furious! How could he have gone ahead without design direction? How could he possibly know what to build? What if it was wrong or didn't work? He'd have to rewrite all the code!

Turns out, the work he did allowed the team to see some of these ideas much sooner than before. It gave team members a glimpse into the actual product experience and allowed them to quickly iterate their designs to be more usable and feasible. From that moment on, they relaxed the BDUF requirements, especially as the team pushed into features that required animations and new UI patterns.

The irony of the team's document dependency and the "inspiration" it triggered in that one developer was not lost. In fact, at the end of the project, Jeff was given a mock award (Figure 17-1) for inspiring "undocumented creativity" in a teammate.

Even though most Agile teams these days say that they shun the concept of BDUF, we've seen a resurgence in this practice in supposedly Agile environments. This new, sneaky version of BDUF is sometimes called *Agilefall*. (Or Agile-Scrum-Fall, Water-Scrum-Fall, or Wagile. You get the idea.) Agilefall is the combination of an up-front design phase that results in work that is handed off, waterfall style, to an engineering team to then break up into stories and develop in an "agile" way. The argument for this way of working centers on the engineering team's desire to stay the course during implementation and to be able to predict when the work will ship with some degree of confidence. This is done in the name of predictability and efficiency.

The 'Rogue Developer' award for inspiring undocumented creativity in engineers

is hereby granted to:

Jeff Gothelf

for outstanding performance and lasting contribution to
AOL Explorer
Awarded: August 4, 2005

AOL Explorer Team

Figure 17-1. *Jeff's "award" for inspiring undocumented creativity in engineers*

The problem, of course, is that Agilefall removes the collaboration between design and engineering that Lean UX requires to succeed. It ends up forcing teams to create big documentation to communicate design, followed by even lengthier negotiations between designers and developers. Sound familiar? It's BDUF in a new disguise. The waste created with Agilefall is a symptom of a broader management issue that continues to push teams toward fixed scope and fixed deadlines. Engineers rightly feel the only way they can make scope and deadline commitments is if they have a crystal-clear understanding of what needs to be developed, along with a promise that nothing will change. (Never mind that Agile is about embracing change!) Of course, as we know by now, software is complex and unpredictable, and, even with a locked-down design, the ability to predict exactly what will ship and when it will ship is closer to fortune-telling than it is to project management.

If Agilefall is the way your team works, consider amplifying the conversation about managing to outcomes with your stakeholders. By moving the conversation away from fixed time and scope and steering toward customer behavior as a measure of success, the demands to do all the design work up front should begin to disappear.

Shift: Embrace speed first, aesthetics second

Jason Fried, CEO of Basecamp, once said, "Speed first, aesthetics second."

He wasn't talking about compromising quality. He was talking about editing his ideas and process down to the core. In Lean UX, working quickly means generating many artifacts. Don't waste time debating which type of artifact to create, and don't waste time polishing them to perfection. Instead, ask yourself the following:

- Who do I need to communicate with?
- What do I need to get across to them immediately?
- What's the least amount of work I need to do to communicate that to them?

If you're working with a developer who is sitting next to you, a whiteboard sketch might suffice. If an executive is asking detailed product questions, you might need to create a visual mock-up. Customers might require prototypes. Whatever the scenario, create the artifact that will take the least amount of time. Remember, these artifacts are a transient part of the project—like a conversation. Get it done. Get it out there. Discuss. Move on.

Aesthetics—in the visual design sense—are an essential part of a finished product and experience. The fit and finish of these elements make a critical contribution to brand, emotional experience, and professionalism. At the visual design refinement stage of the process, putting the effort to obsess over this layer of presentation makes a lot of sense. However, putting in this level of polish and effort into the early-stage artifacts—wireframes, site maps, workflow diagrams—is (usually) a waste of time.

By sacrificing the perfection of intermediate design artifacts, your team will get to market faster and learn more quickly which elements of the whole experience (design, workflow, copy, content, performance, value propositions, etc.) are working for the users and which aren't. And you'll be more willing to change and rework your ideas if you've put less effort into presenting them.

Shift: Tackle UX debt

It's often the case that teams working in Agile processes do not actually go back to improve the UI of the software. But, as our friend Jeff Patton likes to say, "It's not iteration if you do it only once." Teams need to make a commitment to continuous improvement, and that means not simply refactoring code and addressing technical debt but also reworking and improving UIs. Teams need to embrace the concept of UX debt and make a commitment to continuous improvement of the user experience.

James O'Brien, an interaction designer working in London, describes what happened when his team began tracking UX debt in the same manner that the team used to track technical debt. "The effect was dramatic. Once we presented *rework* as *debt*, all opposition fell away. Not only was there no question of the debt not being paid down, but it was consistently prioritized."[2]

To begin tracking UX debt, you can just create a category of stories in your backlog called UX debt. Sometimes, though, experience problems are not something that a single team can solve—solving bigger problems can require the coordinated effort of many teams. For these larger efforts—experience problems that span large user journeys—try this:

- Create a customer journey map of the current experience.
- Work together with your team to create a second journey map that shows the ideal experience.
- Make these two artifacts clearly visible (on a wall) next to each other.
- Identify teams responsible for portions of that customer journey and invite them to the wall to review the gap between current and desired states.
- Work with these teams to write UX debt stories to go on their backlogs.
- Clearly identify on the journey maps when the current experience has been improved and who is working on other improvements.

Shift: Rethink documentation practices

Depending on the domain you work in, your organization might impose strict documentation standards that meet both internal and regulatory compliance. These documents might not add much or any value for the project while it's in flight, yet the team still has to create them. Many teams struggle to move their projects forward when faced with these regulations. They wait until the documents are complete before beginning the design and implementation of the work, slowing down progress and team learning. Then, when the documents are complete, any adjustment of the work described within them is discouraged because of the documentation overhead that change will drive.

This situation is exactly where, as designer and coach Lane Goldstone put it, you "lead with conversation, and trail with documentation." The basic philosophies and concepts of Lean UX can be executed within these environments— conversation, collaborative problem-solving, sketching, experimentation, and so on—during the early parts of the project life cycle. As hypotheses are proven and design directions solidify, transition from informal documentation

---

2 James O'Brien, interview with Joshua Seiden and Jeff Gothelf, 2012.

practices back to the documentation standard your company requires. Use this documentation for the exact reason your company demands: to capture decision history and inform future teams working on this product. Don't let it hold you up from making the right product decisions.

Shift: Manage up and out

Lean UX gives teams a lot of freedom to pursue effective solutions. It does this by stepping away from a feature road map approach and instead empowers teams to discover the features they think will best serve the business. But abandoning the feature road map has a cost: it removes a key tool that the business uses to coordinate the activity of teams. So with the freedom to pursue your agenda comes a responsibility to communicate that agenda.

You must constantly reach out to members of your organization who are not currently involved in your work to make them aware of what's coming down the pike. This communication will also make you aware of what others are planning and help you to coordinate. Customer service managers, marketers, parallel business units, and sales teams all benefit from knowing what the product organization is up to. By reaching out to them proactively, you allow them to do their jobs better. In turn, they will be far less resistant to the change your product designs are making.

Here are two valuable lessons to ensure smoother validation cycles:

- There are always other departments that are affected by your work. Ignore them at your peril.
- Ensure customers are aware of any significant upcoming changes and provide them the option to opt out (at least temporarily).

CHAPTER 18

Lean UX in an Agency

Much of the focus of this book has been explicitly about making Lean UX work inside a product company or within a product group inside a larger business or organization. While the majority of that advice can be applied in any setting, it's worth calling out explicitly the differences needed to make Lean UX work at an agency.

For the sake of this discussion, when we say "agency," we mean any organization that sells services to a client. This could be a small four-person design studio in Portland, Oregon, or a thousand-person marketing agency in London. What makes Lean UX uniquely challenging in this environment is, in a word, clients. It's difficult for agencies to bring new ways of working to clients that find these ways of working foreign to their culture. Now, in some cases, this will be the exact reason your agency was hired. In others, it will be a foreign approach continuously threatened by corporate antibodies resistant to different ways of working. Either way, it will be difficult.

In this chapter, we'll cover five key elements to consider as you attempt to bring modern ways of working to your company.

What Business Do You Want to Be In?

Agencies are almost always in the deliverables business. They get paid to deliver a design, a prototype, some research, or a working piece of software. This business model conflicts with Lean UX and its focus on outcomes.

The traditional agency business model is simple: clients pay for deliverables—designs, specs, code, PowerPoint decks—not outcomes. The other part of an agency's business model is utilization: you need to keep your people billing.

The need to keep utilization high can lead to processes that encourage functional silos. These, in turn, lead to "project phases" that encourage deliverable-centric work. Selling cross functional teams is great as long as everyone on the team is billable at all times.

If you're going to transition your agency's ways of working to Lean UX, you have to consider both of these challenges. First and foremost, you can no longer exclusively be in the deliverables business. Will you deliver wireframes, prototypes, research, and working software? Of course you will. But these cannot be the measures of your success. They cannot be the criteria that determine whether or not you get paid. Instead, consider transforming the business into a time-and-materials model. You are not selling "an app" or "a design," but instead you are collaborating with your client to find a solution to a customer and business problem the client is having. What is that solution? The truthful answer is, you don't know. Instead, you're going to work together with the client to discover what that solution should be. Lean UX is the perfect process for this discovery and continuous delivery of a solution for your clients.

In order to ensure utilization stays high, sell small teams for finite periods of time with clear renewal clauses. At the agency we ran for four years together, we would propose a four-person team made up of a product manager, a designer, and two developers as an initial team for nearly every project. That team had a fixed cost per week, and we would normally sell a three-month engagement renewable in three-month blocks. This helped us reinforce the mantra of short cycles because the client had an out or a renewal option every quarter. It reduced our risk as well by giving us the option to fire a client who ended up being a bad fit for the way we wanted to work. Also, having a fixed rate for "the team" rather than each individual on that team allowed us to adjust the staffing on that team as the project warranted without having to go to the client for approval.

Determining your business model in advance of an all-in shift to a Lean UX style of working is important because it will also affect your current staff as well as prospective hires. The only asset an agency has is its people. Designers, product managers, software developers, etc., come to work for you because you promise a certain way of working for specific types of clients. If you promise a Lean UX way of working and end up signing clients who won't work this way, your staff will eventually walk away.

Selling Lean UX to Clients Is All About Setting Expectations

Your clients have been hiring agencies for years. Many clients expect to "throw it over the wall" to the agency and then see the results when they're ready. Collaboration between client and agency in this case can be limited to uninformed and unproductive critique that is based on personal bias, politics, and ass-covering. Given the highly collaborative nature of Lean UX, this is obviously not an acceptable relationship. What can you do to get around this?

Every touchpoint you have with existing and prospective clients is an opportunity to set expectations about how working with you is different. It starts with your brand, your marketing, your positioning, and, most tangibly, your website. Design and write it in such a way that there can be no doubt that you work in a way that sets you apart from traditional agencies. Compound those expectations with a consistent output of content on blogs, in publications, and on social media. Ensure people know your agency as "the Lean UX folks." The first time you speak with your client in person, go over how you work with them. If you get lucky enough to pitch them, your ways of working should be clear and up front in the pitch deck.

If you progress into planning engagements, be clear about how you'll work together and why that's so critical to building a customer-centered way of working. If questions come up from the client that indicate they haven't fully digested that your agency isn't going to be an outsourcing partner for them, pause the process and go over your process again. It's so critical to get this across early and often, because once the contract is signed, any radical shift of expectations could come across poorly to your client.

Nobody Wants to Buy Experiments

As you set expectations about what it will be like to work with you, remember this important statement: *nobody wants to buy experiments*. Your clients want apps. They want software. They want design. What they definitely don't want to buy from you is an experiment. Experiments are risky and tend to fail. They're certainly not the market-grade production software that will help your client increase market share or their profitability. At least that's how they see it.

When we first launched our agency, we led with the idea of experiments in our sales process. A client would say, "I have $100,000 for you to build a mobile app for my business." And we'd respond, "Great! We're going to take $10,000 of that and run experiments to figure out exactly how to spend the other $90,000." Without fail, each client who got this pitch would say, "No. Just use the whole budget to build the app. I know my business and my customers. We don't need to experiment."

This was a clear sign that we hadn't properly differentiated ourselves in the market, hadn't set the right expectations with prospects, and were leading with a tactic rather than desired end result.

Experiments are a part of Lean UX, but they're just a tactic. They're part of a process that's designed to create learning, good decision making, and positive outcomes. Leading our sales pitch with the outcome (e.g., "Our process ensures we make the best decisions to help solve your mobile commerce challenge") proved to be a far more successful way of working.

You Made the Sale! Now Navigate Procurement

Sometimes you'll do all the right things. Your website will tell your story. Your sales pitch will resonate. The client will nod their head. We have ourselves a deal! You pat yourself on the back and start dealing with closing the contract, only to hear that phrase that all service providers dread: "OK, let me get our procurement folks on to this."

If you've ever had to deal with the in-house (or, worse, third-party) procurement department of a large organization, then you know how this feels. All the convincing you did with the client doesn't mean anything to the folks who have to approve the contract and the purchase. Without fail, the conversation flips back instantly to "OK, so we're giving you $100,000. What are the specific deliverables we will get in return? And on what date?"

This is another part of the expectation-setting that needs to happen with clients ahead of time. As you start to close the contract, the goal is to move away from fixed-scope and deliverable-based contracts. Instead, create contracts for engagements that are based on simple time-and-materials agreements or, more radically, toward outcome-based contracts. Outcome-based contracts, or value-based pricing contracts, are rare. They list payment as variable based on how much of the outcome the agency can generate. This is often too much risk for a client (and agencies) to take on without an upper limit to the contract.

Whether you choose time-and-materials or outcomes-based contracts, the agency team will become freer to spend its time iterating toward a specific goal. Clients give up the illusion of certainty that a deliverables-based contract offers but gain a freedom to pursue meaningful and high-quality solutions that are defined in terms of outcomes, not feature lists, and that stand a better chance of making their customers more successful.

You're Not an Outsourcing Partner Anymore

Building a Lean UX process with your clients means that you are not their outsourcing agency anymore. You are their collaboration partner, working toward solving a business problem. Your role is not to augment the client's staff or take on a share of work that they cannot pursue in-house. Your role is to make the client an active partner of your team. Your client needs to understand this too. They will come to stand-ups. They will be involved in decision making on a regular basis. They will take part in product discovery efforts. In our agency, we made very few of the product backlog prioritization decisions. This was the client's explicit responsibility. The only way they could do this effectively was to be present at daily stand-ups, participate with the team in their learning activities, and be present at status updates and decision-making meetings. We took it further and insisted that the client set up shop in our studio for the duration of the engagement. Why? To remove them from daily distractions, put them in a more creative space, and remind them that we're working together as a team.

These relationship expectations need to be in your contract. Your client must commit to this high level of engagement if Lean UX is going to work. Remember that your goal is to build shared understanding. If the client isn't present for the discovery work, the synthesis, and the decision making, then you have to start documenting everything for them, sending it over for approvals, and waiting for that feedback before moving forward. This would bring us back to the traditional agency style of working.

We once had a financial services client agree to all of our terms for working together. They signed the contract and promptly set up shop in our office. They brought in their Windows machines (hey, we were a Mac shop) and from the get-go attempted to re-create their culture inside our studio. They created every obstacle possible to keep us from meeting with their customers. They limited our access to deployment servers and essentially kept us from being able to do the work we'd agreed to in the contract. Eight weeks in, we raised our hands to pause the process. We met with the client and raised concerns that the ways of working we had agreed to were being met with stiff resistance. The client told us there was nothing they could do about it. We wrapped things up neatly in the next two weeks and fired that client. It wasn't that we couldn't continue working in the ways they wanted. It was just that if we did, we risked losing our team due to the client's behavior. That was unacceptable to us.

A Quick Note About Development Partners and Third-Party Vendors

In agency relationships, software development teams (either at the agency, at the client, or working as a third party) are often treated as outsiders and often brought in at the end of a design phase. It's imperative that you change this: development partners must participate through the life of the project—and not simply as passive observers. Instead, you should seek to have software development begin as early as possible. Again, you are looking to create a deep and meaningful collaboration with the entire project team—and to do that, you must actually be working side by side with the developers.

Third-party software development vendors pose a big challenge to Lean UX methods. If a portion of your work is outsourced to a third-party vendor—regardless of the location of the vendor—the Lean UX process is more likely to break down. This is because the contractual relationship with these vendors can make the flexibility that Lean UX requires difficult to achieve.

When working with third-party vendors, try to create projects based on time and materials. This will make it possible for you to create a flexible relationship with your development partner. You will need this in order to respond to the changes that are part of the Lean UX process. Remember, you are building software to learn, and that learning will cause your plans to change. Plan for that change and structure your vendor relationships around it.

When selecting partners, remember that many outsourced development shops are oriented toward production work and see rework as a problem rather than a learning opportunity. When seeking partners for Lean UX work, look for teams willing to embrace experimentation and iteration and who clearly understand the difference between prototyping-to-learn and developing-for-production.

Wrapping Up

Working as a service provider creates different challenges for implementing Lean UX. Remember that this is as much of a cultural shift for your agency as it is a business model shift. It will change not only how you sell but how and who you hire. It's imperative to set expectations with your clients that your ways of working will challenge their notion of working with an agency. A little creativity and a dash of trust can make the contract and procurement process more successful. Finally, a bad client is a bad client regardless of how you're working together. Ensuring the integrity of your team is your topmost priority.

CHAPTER 19

A Last Word

After the first edition of *Lean UX* was released, we were pleased to start getting feedback from readers. After all, Lean UX is all about listening to your users—so we wanted to understand what the "users" of the book had to say. Readers had *lots* to say (thank you!), but one theme emerged from all the others and has stayed persistent over the years. This theme has to do with the need to grow organizations and processes that can really embrace this way of working.

We know that working with Lean UX requires changes. What we didn't understand clearly until we heard from readers is that the changes fall into two categories: changes readers could make for themselves, and changes that required leaders to get involved—leaders who might not want to change, for whatever reasons.

Our readers told us: *Look, we can make certain kinds of changes ourselves, but for other changes, we need to rely on shifting our leader's attitudes. We need to change things beyond ourselves—we need to change the way our organization itself works.*

Now, changing an organization, even a small one, is a big challenge. It's a challenge that most designers and product people have little training or experience trying to enact. Even people seasoned in the field of organizational development know that changing organizations is hard. So it can feel overwhelming. And that's what we heard from our readers. They wanted to know how to change, and they didn't know where to start. They wanted help.

Kind of a bummer, huh?

Well listen: the point of this chapter is not to make you feel hopeless. We firmly believe that people, teams, and companies can change. What's more, we believe that you can use Lean UX to help you make these changes! In addition to helping teams learn Lean UX, we've spent the years since the first edition came out working on these kinds of transformation problems, and we've seen firsthand that change is possible.

Now, the whys and hows and wheres of organizational transformation are beyond the scope of this book, but we want to offer you a starting point.

The Product that Makes the Product

In the words of our friend Barry O'Reilly, a product development organization is "the product that makes the product." In other words, you can approach organizational development using many of the same tools you use for product development. And we firmly believe that you can use the methods of Lean UX in the service of organizational development.

What change do you want to make in your organization? Can you describe the change in terms of the outcome you seek? Maybe you want to make research more collaborative. Your outcome might be: *on future research projects, ensure every team member participates in at least one direct customer interview session*. Or maybe you want to change the way work is assigned to your team. Your outcome might be: *in the next quarter, half of the epics we work on will be defined by a user outcome rather than a feature list*.

Guess what: you're using Lean UX! Now, how are you going to make these changes? Well, you're going to want to try a number of experiments until you find the right way to achieve your outcome. Think of these experiments as *minimum viable process*.

So, while you may not have authority to completely change the way your organization works, there's nothing that's stopping you from enlisting a small group of willing collaborators and using the tools of Lean UX to start creating the organization that you want. You will have to start designing new things (like work processes) for new people (stakeholders, peers, collaborators), but you can do that, right? Yes, you can do that.

We've been so pleased to see so many teams adopting these methods over the years, and we're positive that you can do it too. And, as always, we're excited to hear from you. Good luck on your Lean UX journey, and let us know how it's going!

As we said at the start of this book: please keep in touch and share your thoughts. Reach out to us at *jeff@jeffgothelf.com* and *josh@joshuaseiden.com*. We always look forward to hearing from you.

Index

test what you've got, 148
finish line for work (see "done" rede-
fined)
Flickr fake feature offer, 94
foundations of Lean UX, 7
   Agile software development, 8
   Lean Startup, 9
   user experience design, 8
Fried, Jason, 200
Frog Design company, 128

G

GE Software design systems, 128-131
   GE Digital from GE Software, 129
   Industrial Internet Design System, 128
   Predix design system, 129
geographically distributed teams, 131
   test sessions to remote team members,
      143
get out of the building, 18
   collaborative discovery for, 138
      example, 140
get out of your head, 18
Goldstone, Lane, 201
González, Victor M., 145
Gothelf, Jeff, 181
greenfield projects, xxv

H

hardcoded prototypes, 103
hero-based design, 192
human behavior (see customer behavior)
Human Interface Guidelines (Apple), 125
Hurston, Zora Neale, 137
hypotheses
   about, 77
      compelling hypotheses, 78
   Agile user stories versus, 81
   design sprints, 123
   Design Studio output, 75
   facilitating the Canvas exercise, 79-80
      what to watch out for, 83
   Kaplan–university partnerships, 112
   learning about risks of, 85
   newsletter example MVP, 88
   outcome-based road maps, 178
   prioritizing, 81

subscription service prototype MVP,
   105
template for, 78
validating quickly via conversations,
   141
Hypothesis Prioritization Canvas (HPC),
   82

I

IDEO design firm, 8
IIDS (Industrial Internet Design System),
   128
impacts as key performance indicators
   business outcomes, 47
   business problem statements, 42
   impact metrics, 51
   outcome-to-impact mapping, 51
      what to watch out for, 53
   website meeting example, 23
implementing Lean UX
   about, 187
   adjustments
      agency culture, 193
      Big Design Up Front, 188, 198
      competencies over roles, 195
      development partners, 194, 197,
         207
      distributed teams, 196
      documentation practices, 201
      "done" redefined, 193
      hero-based design, 118, 192
      humility embraced, 190
      managers implementing change,
         194
      managing up and out, 202
      new skills embraced, 190
      outcomes, not output, 197
      small teams, 196
      speed first, aesthetics second, 200
      tackling UX debt, 200
      third-party vendors, 197
      workspaces open and collabora-
        tive, 191
   culture adjustments, 189
   leaders' attitudes shifted, 209
   process adjustments, 189
   team organization adjustments, 189

(see also customer feedback)
definition, xxvi
GE Software User Experience Team, 128-131
get out of the building, 18
collaborative discovery for, 138
Hypothesis Prioritization Canvas, 82
UX debt, 200

V
Validately prototype, 109
validation
iterative nature, 27
outcomes, 27
proto-personas, 59-61
prototype validating product, 109
quick hypothesis validation via conversations, 141
vendors of software development, 194, 197, 207

W
W. K. Kellogg Foundation, 24
waste removed, 14
website MVP examples
collaborative design informal approach, 119
fake features, 94
Kaplan–university partnerships, 110
landing page, 92
newsletter offer, 88
search logs to capture feedback, 155
Taproot Foundation online, 97
Weinberg, Alla, 134
Weiss, Lee, 110
Wizard of Oz for MVP mechanics, 96
Amazon Echo example, 96
Taproot Foundation example, 97

Z
Zeratsky, John, 121

About the Authors

Jeff Gothelf helps organizations build better products and executives build the cultures that build better products. He is coauthor of the award-winning book *Lean UX* and the Harvard Business Review Press book *Sense & Respond* as well as the self-published *Lean Vs. Agile Vs. Design Thinking* (S&R Press) and *Forever Employable* (Gothelf Corp.). Starting off as a software designer, Jeff now works as a coach, consultant and keynote speaker helping companies bridge the gaps between business agility, digital transformation, product management and human-centred design. Most recently Jeff cofounded Sense & Respond Press, a publishing house for practical business books for busy executives.

Josh Seiden is a designer, author, and coach who works with teams to create great products and services. He helps teams solve real problems for customers and create value for businesses. He also works as a coach to help teams improve the way they work, build more effective collaborations, and enjoy the journey of product development. He helps companies create the culture, processes and practices to do great work. He's a cofounder of Sense & Respond Press, a micro-publisher that creates short, beautiful books on innovation, digital transformation, and product management. In addition to *Lean UX*, he's the author of *Outcomes Over Output* (S&R Press) and coauthor of *Sense & Respond* (Harvard Business Review Press).